MULTILEVEL BUSINESS ENGLISH PROGRAMME

—*Course Book*—
Intermediate

Ian Badger

Pete Menzies

PHOENIX
ELT

incorporating
PRENTICE HALL MACMILLAN

New York London Toronto Sydney Tokyo Singapore

Published 1996 by Phoenix ELT
Campus 400, Spring Way
Maylands Avenue, Hemel Hempstead
Hertfordshire, HP2 7EZ

A division of Prentice Hall International (UK) Ltd

Published 1994 by Macmillan Publishers Ltd.

© 1996 Illustrations International Book Distributors Ltd

Printed and bound in Hong Kong

British Library Cataloguing in Publication Data
A catalogue record for this book is available from the British Library

ISBN 0 13 253774 5

5   4   3   2
99 98 97 96

Produced by **AMR**

Acknowledgements

The authors and publishers would particularly like to thank the following who kindly gave permission to interview members of their staff:

Lansing Linde Ltd
McDonald's Golden Arches Restaurants Ltd

The authors and publishers wish to thank the following for permission to use copyright material:

Cameron Balloons Ltd for material from their brochures; Clerical Medical Investment Group for material from an advertisement; The Guardian for 'French Ban is Case of Laissez-Fumer', *The Guardian*, 31.10.92; The Controller of Her Majesty's Stationery Office for data from 'General Household Survey 1991'; McGraw-Hill Publications for the cartoon 'I say! Weren't we in prison together?' from *International Management* Jul/Aug 1988; National Westminster Bank for the Pharos application form; The Royal Air Force Benevolent Fund Enterprises for material from their International Air Tattoo 1991 brochure advertising 'The Skyhigh Club'; Times Newspapers Ltd. for the table, 'Charting 12 Years of King-Size Profits at British Airways', *Sunday Times*, 29.2.93 and 'Who Gets the Perks', *The Times*, 25.6.91; Young & Co's Brewery PLC for material from their Report and Accounts 1993.

The authors and publisher wish to acknowledge with thanks the following photographic sources: 73, Air France; 91, British Airways PLC; 61, Cable & Wireless Visual Resource; 40, 41, Cameron Balloons Ltd; 75, Copthorne Hotels; 45, Greg Evans International; 63, Images Colour Library; 24, Photothèque EDF (top, Marc Morceau; bottom, Michel Brigaud); 81, Pictor International; 13, 19, 22, 27, 49, 55, 57, 64, 83, 87, Stuart Boreham; 50, Sutcliffe Catering; 15, 21, 29, 37, 42, 53, 58, 69, 79, The Image Bank; 31, 77, 88, The Telegraph Colour Library; 35, Times Syndication; 47, 67, 85, Tony Stone Images.

Every effort has been made to trace all the copyright holders, but if any have been inadvertently overlooked, the publishers will be pleased to make the necessary arrangement at the first opportunity.

The authors would like to thank the following for their considerable help in realising this project:

Sheena Forrester; Virginia Doyle; Annette Sloan; Geraldine Badger; the BMES team (Valerie Lambert; Sarah Cheetham, Jan Borgen); Rosemary Upton; the Macmillan team (Catherine Gray, Susan Holden, Adrian Soar, Anne Young, Chester Krone); the AMR team (Anne Murray-Robertson, Sharon Lunn, Ann Miller); and Gerald Ramshaw, for doing the recordings.

Special thanks also to 'students' from United Paper Mills, Sunds Defibrator and the International Maritime Organisation for their valuable assistance and feedback.

CONTENTS

CONTENTS CHART

UNIT	ACTIVITY	SKILLS	LANGUAGE
3 PERSONNEL **B** **Personal background**	giving personal background information	**Listening:** giving personal news **Reading/Writing:** an advertisement	the Present Perfect tense *have/had to* *still* and *yet*
3 PERSONNEL **C** **Conditions of work**	talking about fringe benefits	**Listening:** what staff were doing at the time of a fire **Reading/Writing:** features of a good office environment	the Past Perfect tense the Past Continuous tense *too/enough + to/for (too heavy to lift, not enough space for us all,* etc.) some office equipment/ furniture
3 PERSONNEL **D** **Job descriptions**	making suggestions and recommendations talking about qualifications	**Listening:** talking about a job **Reading/Writing:** a profile of a management consultant describing what someone looks like	replying to negative sentences recommending and suggesting (*Have you thought of...?*) criticising (*I don't think you should...*) wish (*I wish you wouldn't...*) describing appearance and dress the opposites of adjectives (*safe/unsafe,* etc.)
4 PRODUCTS **B** **The products you make/use**	ordering products	**Listening:** talking about products and their key selling points a follow-up phone call to arrange a meeting **Reading/Writing:** a product enquiry	*used to* (*You used to supply...*) adverbs in phrases (*highly competitive,* etc.) numbers and symbols materials and substances (*steel, concrete,* etc.)
4 PRODUCTS **C** **Product descriptions**	giving a short product presentation	**Listening:** describing a production process **Reading/Writing:** product information from a brochure	the Present Perfect Continuous tense the Present Simple Passive tense indirect questions (*Do you know whether...?*) describing a process (*First..., then...,* etc.) shapes (*square, rectangular,* etc.) imperial measurements
4 PRODUCTS **D** **Compliments and complaints**	expressing satisfaction and dissatisfaction with a product	**Listening:** causes for complaint **Reading/Writing:** a notice of product recall a letter of complaint	relative pronouns (*which, whose,* etc.) the order of adjectives *need + -ing* (*It needs mending.*) causes for complaint (*dented, scratched,* etc.)

UNIT	ACTIVITY	SKILLS	LANGUAGE
5 SERVICES **B The services you provide/use**	considering whether to lease or purchase	**Listening:** reasons for using a service saying if a service is handled in-house or subcontracted **Reading/Writing:** an advertisement for a fax machine	*to have/get something done* expressing necessity (*need, must*, etc.) reflexive pronouns (*myself*, etc.) *own* (*We handle our own cleaning.*) payment times (*weekly, per week*, etc.)
5 SERVICES **C Dealing with problems**	making and dealing with complaints	**Listening:** sorting out a problem **Reading/Writing:** an exchange of letters	the Past tense of modal verbs (*You should have...*) *due to, on account of*, etc. apologising accepting and rejecting apologies
5 SERVICES **D Service companies**	researching a catering service	**Listening:** speakers from different service industries **Reading/Writing:** details of a catering company a case of recycling	correcting misunderstandings (*must have*, etc.) *such as, like*, etc. fees and charges (*What do you charge for...?*) jobs in service industries
6 ENTERTAINING **B Business hospitality**	inviting a client out	**Listening:** entertaining business visitors **Reading/Writing:** cultural 'Do's and 'Don't's	adverbs of frequency giving advice (*You should always...*, etc.) *mustn't, needn't* and *don't have to* *was/were going/hoping/ planning to* *prefer* and *would rather*
6 ENTERTAINING **C Hotels and restaurants**	entertaining guests in a hotel quoting from a document	**Listening:** ordering a meal in a restaurant **Reading/Writing:** a restaurant menu an article about who should pay the bill	reported speech *say* v. *tell* *speak* v. *talk* food vocabulary making a toast and leaving a tip
6 ENTERTAINING **D Corporate entertaining**	arranging hospitality for customers	**Listening:** booking a hospitality package **Reading/Writing:** publicity brochures for a flying display and a golf tournament	the spelling and position of adverbs comparative adverbs the Simple Present tense for timetables (*It opens at 8 am.*) more on suggestions (*I would recommend...*) some sports vocabulary (*Good shot!*)

UNIT	ACTIVITY	SKILLS	LANGUAGE
7 MEETINGS **B Setting up a meeting**	preparing an agenda setting up and rearranging a meeting	**Listening:** last-minute changes **Reading/Writing:** an exchange of faxes sample agendas	*had better* *to be able to* *look as if/though and sound as if/though* punctuation
7 MEETINGS **C Procedure**	holding a meeting	**Listening:** excerpts from meetings in progress suggesting items for an agenda **Reading/Writing:** an article on smoking in the workplace	phrases used in meetings the Second Conditional expressing agreement and disagreement referring to documents (*In line 3, it says...*)
7 MEETINGS **D Follow-up**	checking action steps	**Listening:** a follow-up phone call **Reading/Writing:** written follow-up to a meeting a list of action steps	verbs followed by the infinitive more reported speech action points (*AB to call CD,* etc.)
8 TRAVEL **B Arranging a visit**	checking the details of an itinerary	**Listening:** directions from an airport **Reading/Writing:** a letter of introduction directions from an airport in reply to a letter an itinerary	the Future Continuous tense (*I'll be working in Boston...*) *while, during* and *for* more directions (*Follow the signs to...*)
8 TRAVEL **C Abroad on business**	handling common travel situations (airport check-in, car hire, etc.)	**Listening:** short dialogues at a hotel check-in, a ticket office, a filling station and a car hire desk **Reading/Writing:** advice on jet lag	*when, as soon as, while, before,* etc. in future sentences *easy/difficult to,* etc. some travel vocabulary
8 TRAVEL **D Reporting back**	reporting back on a trip commenting on hotels	**Listening:** talking about a trip **Reading/Writing:** an overview of a market a hotel assessment form	*in case* (*in case it rains*) *how far...?* and *a long way* *how long...?* and *a long time* rankings (*second largest,* etc.) points of the compass some acronyms (OPEC, GATT, etc.)

UNIT	ACTIVITY	SKILLS	LANGUAGE
9 MONEY AND FINANCE **B Personal finances**	discussing and comparing personal expenditure reporting a theft	**Listening:** talking about personal expenditure **Reading/Writing:** a profit and loss account a story of a false insurance claim	*same as, different from* and *similar to* fractions and multiples in comparisons (*half/twice as much as...*) *do* and *did* for emphasis some common financial vocabulary some profit and loss account terms some insurance terms
9 MONEY AND FINANCE **C Company finances**	comparing company performance	**Listening:** an annual review of a company **Reading/Writing:** a balance sheet with explanations	further revision of the Passive balance sheet headings some common business abbreviations (*a/c, b/f,* etc.)
9 MONEY AND FINANCE **D Payment**	explaining non-payment of an invoice	**Listening:** giving reasons for not paying requesting payment and giving invoice details **Reading/Writing:** a letter requesting payment and a letter of reply an invoice	*unless* and *provided/ providing* *apparently, it seems that,* etc. *each* and *every* more mathematical terms
10 PRESENTATIONS **B Preparation**	setting up a room for a presentation	**Listening:** discussing equipment needed **Reading/Writing:** making notes on a text a company statement	verb + preposition + -ing (*I apologise for being late.*) giving preferences (*I don't mind...*) *to be used to* and *to get used to* some equipment for presentations
10 PRESENTATIONS **C Facts and figures**	describing a graph locating information on a page updating information	**Listening:** plotting a graph **Reading/Writing:** a fact sheet on a major retailer	verb + infinitive or -ing more numbers (*one in three,* etc.) *average* (*to average, on average,* etc.) social groups (*professionals, manual workers,* etc.)
10 PRESENTATIONS **D Some company presentations**	giving a presentation	**Listening:** two short company presentations **Reading/Writing:** notes on a company's history	*because, as* and *since* *so* and *therefore* *although, even though, in spite of* (*the fact that*), etc. phrases used in presentations

INTRODUCTION

... A MULTI-LEVEL COURSE ...

Welcome to the *Macmillan Business English Programme*, a comprehensive, multi-level course of English for business people, which takes learners from false beginner to advanced level. The core course is supplemented by optional specialised modules.

Each level of the core course consists of:

- a Course Book, providing between 80 and 120 hours of class work;
- a Self-Study Pack, including extensive listening materials, published in monolingual or bilingual editions as appropriate;
- a Trainer's Pack, which includes a Trainer's Guide with answers and tapescripts, and Supplementary Exercises for each unit, which can be used in class or for homework;
- recordings for class use.

... CENTRAL IDEAS ...

Ideas that are central to the programme:

- The course follows a progressive and comprehensive grammar syllabus, with a stress on the effective use of grammar for clear communication. It therefore provides the business learner with a practical and realistic alternative to general English courses at all levels.
- The course reflects the fact that English is a language which is used for international communication. The learner is thus presented with a range of native and non-native speaker English.
- The course is not set within a specific business context. This gives the material a flexibility of use that allows trainers and learners to apply the material to their specific business situations.

... PROBLEMS BUSINESS LEARNERS MEET ...

Business people who want to improve their English often meet the following problems:

- *Time available for classes is limited, so progress is slow.*
  In this programme, each Course Book unit has a parallel unit in the Self-Study Pack, which provides the opportunity to revise and practise further. This integrated self-study facility means that learners are free to supplement class work as necessary.
- *Conflicting work commitments make attendance irregular.*
  Each unit in the Self-Study Pack includes notes which underline and summarise the points made in the parallel Course Book lesson. The Self-Study Pack can therefore be used to catch up on classes missed.
- *The content of courses is either too general or set in a business environment that is not relevant.*
  The *Macmillan Business English Programme* consists of a core course supplemented by specialised modules. The core course presents the grammar and vocabulary needed by any business person wishing to use English for work or work-related social activities; the language of specific business areas is dealt with in the supplementary modules. The authors have extensive experience of working in companies, and they have taken care to ensure that the language in the course is rooted in the real business world.

... EQUIVALENCE ...

Learners, and companies which sponsor language training, may be interested in checking levels of attainment. The following table shows how the *Macmillan Business English Programme* compares with some existing examinations in Business English.

Macmillan Business English Programme	University of Oxford Delegacy of Local Examinations	London Chamber of Commerce and Industry		University of Cambridge Local Examinations Syndicate/Royal Society of Arts	International Certificate Conference
Elementary Level		SEFIC[2] Preliminary			
Pre-Intermediate Level		SEFIC Threshold	EFB[3] One		
Intermediate Level	OIBEC[1] First Level	SEFIC Intermediate	EFB Two		CEBP[5]
Higher Intermediate Level	OIBEC Executive Level		EFB Three	CEIBT[4]	
Advanced Level		SEFIC Advanced			

[1]OIBEC (Oxford International Business English Certificate)

[2]SEFIC (Spoken English for Industry and Commerce)

[3]EFB (English for Business)

[4]CEIBT (Certificate in English for International Business and Trade)

[5]CEBP (Certificate in English for Business Purposes)

(Secretarial staff may be interested in the Pitman exams for reading and writing. For the addresses of the various examination boards, see page 12.)

... THIS BOOK ...

The intermediate level of the *Macmillan Business English Programme* will be appropriate for you if you have studied English for perhaps three to six years at school and/or college. You will probably be able to use the language with a fair degree of fluency. However, although you will be able to 'get by' in most situations requiring English, your level of fluency and grammatical accuracy may not be as high as your work demands.

This book will help you to improve your ability to use English in a wide range of business and business-related social situations. It will also be of interest if you have a higher level of general English, but need, specifically, to improve your English for business communication.

... STUDY TIPS ...

- Make time for your English studies. Approach them with the same level of commitment that you would any other project in your work.
- Find the study pattern that works best for you. In our view, 'little and often' is more effective than occasional long sessions.
- Keep an organised study file. Make sure that the language that is most relevant to your needs is clearly highlighted.
- Ensure that the language taught relates back to your area of business. If there are terms you need which are not included in the material, consult your trainer and make thorough notes.
- Consider forming a study group. Meet outside class time to work through exercises together and to encourage each other.
- Make use of dictionaries and other reference books. Useful business dictionaries are the *English Business Dictionary* (Peter Collin Publishing), the *Longman Dictionary of Business English*, J. H. Adam (Longman), and the *Oxford Dictionary of Business English* (Oxford University Press). Other books you may find useful: *An Introduction to Business Organisation and Practice*, a module in the *Macmillan Business English Programme*; *Practical English Usage*, Michael Swan (Oxford University Press); *English Grammar in Use*, Raymond Murphy (Cambridge University Press).

... ABOUT THE AUTHORS ...

Ian Badger is a partner in Business and Medical English Services, Bristol, a consultancy specialising in the provision of language training for business and the medical professions. He has extensive experience of working with companies to develop courses and systems of language training, both in-company and off-site.

Pete Menzies is the author of a number of English language teaching text books, including a prize-winning series of case studies for business learners. He runs the in-service English programme at the International Maritime Organisation, London. He studied accountancy with Singleton Fabian in the City of London.

Addresses

University of Oxford Delegacy of Local Examinations, Ewert House, Ewert Place, Summertown, Oxford OX2 7BZ (Tel: 0865 54291; Fax: 0865 510085)

London Chamber of Commerce and Industry, Languages Section, Marlowe House, Station Road, Sidcup, Kent (Tel: 081 302 0261; Fax: 081 302 4169)

University of Cambridge Local Examinations Syndicate (UCLES), Syndicate Buildings, 1 Hills Road, Cambridge CB1 2EU (Tel: 0223 61111; Fax 0223 460278)

International Certificate Conference (ICC), Holzhausenstr. 21 D-6000 Frankfurt 1 GERMANY (Tel: 069 1540 0547; Fax: 069 1540 0538)

Pitman Examinations Institute, Catteshall Manor, Godalming, Surrey GU7 IUU (Tel: 04868 5311)

CONTACTS

A Introduction

1 CONTENTS

2 REVISION

1 Revise the alphabet – see the telephone alphabets on page 93. Spell your name, the name of your company, the names of people and places that are important to you, etc.

2 Revise definite and indefinite articles (*the* and *a/an*). Fill in the gaps with *the*, *a*, *an* or –.

a I'm __a__ sales executive.
b I'm in __the__ sales department.
c I'm in _____ Sales.
d We are __the__ biggest department in __the__ company.
e We have __a__ European sales force of 300 people.

3 Revise ways of making contact.

How do you greet someone you haven't seen for a while?
How do you introduce yourself?
How do you ask to speak to someone on the phone?
What do you say when the person you want isn't there, and you want to leave a message?

4 Revise *so* and *such (a)*. Fill in the gaps. Then give further examples.

a We have __so__ much work at the moment that everyone is having to work overtime.
b This is __such a__ busy time of the year.
c We have __such__ demanding customers!

5 Can you use this telephone vocabulary? Put the terms in sentences or exchanges.

| engaged | call back | put through | extension | line | hold on |

6 Revise *much*, *many* and *a lot (of)*. Fill in the gaps. Then give further examples.

a I have so __much__ work to do.
b I have so __many__ things to do.
c Have you got __a lot__ to do this afternoon?
d There weren't __a lot__ people at the meeting.
e He's under __a lot of__ pressure.

7 Telling the time: in how many ways can you say these times?

14.15   18.45   19.10   05.00   11.30

B Contacts at work

1 ACTIVITY

Work in pairs. Find out about your partner's language needs.

Questionnaire	every day	twice a week	once a week	every now and then
How often do you use English...				
...with colleagues?				
...with customers/clients?				
...with superiors/bosses?				
...with employees who report to you?				
...with travel agents?				
...with friends?				
...other?				
How often do you use English to...				
...make arrangements?				
...welcome visitors?				
...talk on the phone?				
...write faxes?				
...other?				
How often do you have communication problems because of...				
...time differences?				
...different working hours?				
...local accents?				
...cultural differences?				
...other?				

2 LISTENING

Time differences

1 In pairs, practise talking about time differences. Make calls to these cities. (There is a time map on page 138.)

a Seoul   **b** Istanbul   **c** Moscow   **d** Colombo

e.g. We open at 8 am, that's four in the afternoon Korean time. We're eight hours behind you.

They arrive at eleven o'clock Eastern Standard Time. That's 2 pm your time. You are three hours ahead.

2 Mr Harvey, the UK agent for a Finnish company that makes medical instruments, talks about good and bad aspects of communicating with his supplier. Listen and answer the questions.

a What is the 'small and practical' area where there is room for improvement?
b How could the situation be improved?
c What is 'absolutely essential'?
d What is the general level of English like in the company?

3 LANGUAGE POINTS

Revise articles and *some/any* (see page 93).

1 Notice these examples:

We need to arrange <u>a time</u> to meet.
Do you know <u>the time</u> of the meeting?
<u>Time</u> is against us.
Have you got <u>any time</u> this afternoon?
I've got <u>some free time</u> tomorrow.

2 Complete the sentences with *a*, *the*, *some*, *any* or *–*. In some cases, there is more than one possibility.

a Have you got _____ today's newspaper?
b Have you seen _____ paper?
c I bought _____ interesting magazine today.
d We need _____ new equipment.

e Have you heard _____ latest news?
f We haven't got _____ problems with _____ new machine.
g My assistant never does _____ work.
h _____ standard of his work is very poor.
i I have _____ information for you.
j I've got _____ new job.

Seasons and festivals

3 Work in pairs. Discuss which of these festivals you celebrate and which your overseas contacts celebrate.

When do they occur?
Do they cause any inconvenience?
How do you celebrate them?
How do you greet someone on that day?

Christmas	Chinese New Year	Ramadan
Passover	May Day	Boxing Day
Thanksgiving	Easter	Independence Day etc.

4 ACTIVITY

Beginning and ending telephone calls

▲ 'I can't really talk now.'

Practise short phone conversations in pairs. Use the table as necessary.

Beginning a call

Hello, is that [Esther]? Are you in the middle of something? Are you busy?	Have you got a minute? Can you talk? Is this a good/bad time?
I can't really talk now. I'm a bit tied up at the moment. Can I call you back this afternoon?	It's a good time. I'm not doing anything. Go ahead.
Of course, what time will you call? Sure, can you call before 5.30?	I'm calling about [Thursday's meeting]. It's about...

Ending a call

Is there anything else (we need to talk about)?
Have we covered everything?
Is that everything?

No, I don't think so. Yes, I think so. I hope so.	There is one other point. (There's just) one more thing...

(Later...)

I'm afraid I must go [soon].
I've got [a meeting at 3.15].
I have to...

(So) thanks for calling. I'll [call you next week]. (Good)bye.	OK, I'll [be in touch]. OK, I'll wait to [hear from you]. Give my regards to [Max].

5 LISTENING

Taking and leaving messages
Say, tell and *ask* (see page 94)

Tuesday, 3.15. Mat Wiersma called. He wants you to call him as soon as you get back. Lorna.

1 Listen to the telephone calls and tick [✔] the explanations you hear.
2 Listen to the messages the callers leave. Write notes for the people concerned.

- not in yet   [ ]
- having a coffee break   [ ]
- at lunch   [ ]
- gone home   [ ]
- ill or on sick leave   [ ]
- on holiday   [ ]
- in a meeting   [ ]
- with some visitors   [ ]

- in the building somewhere   [ ]
- on another number   [ ]
- away this week   [ ]
- out at the moment   [ ]
- not available   [ ]
- not at his/her desk   [ ]

C Developing contacts

1 READING

A letter of introduction

1 Read the letter and fill in the gaps, using the terms in the box. What information would you include in a letter of introduction?

> branches   colleague   confident   next month
> personality   relationships   responsible for   to lose

Santoro Consumer Electronics S.r.L.
Via Fa di Bruno 37   016739 Roma
Tel. 0093 – 739 – 21049   Fax. 0092 – 739 – 076037

Wednesday 24th February 19..
Ref. RS.PV1

Dear Benjamin,

I am writing to introduce my (**a**) _____ Ms Magda Grega, who will be joining your data processing systems planning department (**b**) _____ . As you probably know, she has been (**c**) _____ office automation within the whole group, and we will be sorry (**d**) _____ her. She has had an important role in co-ordinating dealings between the hardware and software suppliers and the company (**e**) _____ , and has established excellent (**f**) _____ throughout the company.

On a personal note, she is a likeable and energetic person with an outgoing (**g**) _____ , who can be tough when necessary. I am (**h**) _____ that you will enjoy working with her.

With best wishes,

Rakesh Singh

Rakesh Singh
Deputy IT Director (Europe)

Adjectives describing positive personal qualities

2 Check that you know these adjectives. Then write a letter introducing a colleague and referring to his/her personal qualities.

> cheerful   clever   competent   efficient   energetic   experienced
> friendly   hard-working   helpful   highly-qualified   intelligent
> likeable   outgoing   quiet   reliable   self-confident   tough   warm

2 LANGUAGE POINTS

Revise *much, many* and *a lot (of)* (see page 95).

1 Complete these sentences. In some cases, there will be more than one possibility.

a I have got quite _____ to do this afternoon.
b I haven't got very _____ to do tomorrow.
c There are _____ things to arrange.
d Are there _____ more calls to make? Yes, quite _____ .
e There isn't very _____ enthusiasm for the project.
f There aren't _____ days till the deadline.
g Have you got _____ more work to do? No, not _____ .

Revise *several, (a) few* and *(a) little*
(see page 95).

2   Complete these sentences so that they are true.

e.g. I know several <u>people who could help you.</u>

a   We have very little _____ .
b   There are quite a few _____ .
c   We receive very few _____ .
d   Would you like a little _____ ?
e   There are several _____ .
f   There were a few _____ .
g   We have quite a few _____ .

Revise *so* and *such (a)* (see page
95).

3   Complete the sentences using *so* and *such (a)*.

a   They have _____ good contacts that...
b   Everyone was _____ helpful that...
c   It would be difficult to find _____ comfortable hotel in my country.
d   There are _____ many people I need to see.
e   Why was the customer _____ angry?
f   We gave him _____ good deal that...
g   How did you get _____ cheap deal?
h   I have had _____ much work to do recently.

3 LISTENING

Time references (see page 95)

Listen to people following up a new contact. Match the time of the first
meeting with the time of the next one.

a   last Tuesday   i   next month
b   a couple of days ago   ii   in three weeks' time
c   the week before last   iii the month after next
d   a week last Friday   iv   a week on Monday

4 ACTIVITY

Exploring contacts

Work in pairs, using the language boxes below as a guide.

Contacts in different geographical locations

Who do you know in [Lodz]?
Have you got any contacts in [Poland]?
Do you know anyone in [Poznan]?
I've got a few contacts in [Krakow].
I'll give you a letter of introduction.

Contacts in different professions/occupations

Do you know a good [lawyer]?
What is your [accountant] like?
Do you have a good [tax advisor]?
Who is the best [tour operator] in town?
I can recommend [the people] we use.
He/She is good to work with.

Contacts in different businesses and industries

Do you know anyone who sells [photocopiers]?
                    ...who can supply _____ ?
                    ...who deals in _____ ?
                    ...who works in [a bank]?
                    ...who works in [the construction business]?
I know a very good [haulage contractor].

D Outside office hours

1 READING AND LISTENING

Problems with arrangements

A fax arrives at Ergo Construction from the Commercial Investment Bank. Read it. Then listen to the recording and answer the questions below. Why is the fax so urgent?

URGENT FAX MESSAGE! PLEASE READ IMMEDIATELY!

I am trying to contact Harry Crew, the head of your legal department, but your switchboard is closed and I do not have his direct number.

This is a matter of urgency because I am meeting him for dinner at seven o'clock to discuss matters of some importance to both our companies, but I do not know the name or address of the restaurant.

If he is still in the building, could you ask him to contact me as soon as possible. If he has left, I would be very grateful if you could call and give me his home number. I am on 0203 437 294.

With thanks,

Fiona Temple

Fiona Temple, Commercial Loans Manager

---

a Who calls Fiona Temple back?
b Does Ms Temple call Harry Crew's home number?
c Where are they meeting?
d Why hasn't Ms Temple got the details?
e How will she get to the meeting place?

2 LANGUAGE POINTS

Requests and offers

1 Note these examples of requests.

Could you (not) tell him I called (please)?
Would you (not) tell him I called (please)?
Would you mind (not) telling him I called (please)?

2 Change the demands into requests.

e.g. Ask her to call me. _Could you ask her to call me?_

a Write this phone number down. _____
b Take this parcel to reception. _____
c Give her a message. _____
d Book my flight tickets. _____
e Don't give anyone my home number. _____
f Don't park there. _____
g Don't phone me tomorrow. _____

3 Note these examples of offers.

Can/Could I get him to ring you in the morning?
Shall I get him to ring you in the morning?
Would you like me to get him to ring you in the morning?
Let me get him to ring you in the morning.

4 Offer to help, using the prompts.

e.g. (take a message) _Can I take a message?_

a (call you next week) _____
b (prepare an agenda for the meeting) _____
c (get in touch with the Beijing office) _____
d (book some theatre tickets for you) _____
e (buy you a drink) _____
f (drive you to the station) _____
g (check the order number) _____

3 LISTENING

Answerphone messages

1 Listen and write down the recorded messages.

TO:
FROM:
MESSAGE:

TO:
FROM:
MESSAGE:

TO:
FROM:
MESSAGE:

TO:
FROM:
MESSAGE:

Offering refreshments

2 Listen and match the speakers to the places.

| an office   an exhibition stand   a car hire office   a bar |

Dialogue a _____   **Dialogue c** _____
Dialogue b _____   **Dialogue d** _____

4 ACTIVITY

Making contact after working hours

Practise getting in touch about arrangements after working hours. Use the table as a guide.

Partner A: You are working late.
Partner B: You are an outside caller. You want to speak to **Partner C**.
Partner C: You have already gone home.

Partner A takes an outside call from **Partner B**.

▲ 'I'm afraid I can't give out a private number.'

| I'm sorry, but I'm afraid the office is closed. You've missed him/her. He/She has gone home. I'm afraid we don't give out private numbers. I'll try and get a message to him/her. | ◀▶ | Do you know how I can get in touch with him/her? Is it possible to get hold of him/her? Do you have his/her home number? Would you mind calling him/her? Would you ask him/her to phone me? |

Partner C calls **Partner B**.

| I'm ringing because I got a message to call you. Where are you? What's the problem? Are you coming? How long will you be? | ◀▶ | I've been trying to contact you. Your office wouldn't give me your number. I don't know how to reach you. What's your address/number? I'll see you in about [20 minutes]. |

Partner C welcomes **Partner B**.

| You made it. It's good to see you. Come and meet _____ . Would you like a drink? What will you have? Ice? / Milk and sugar? | ◀▶ | I'm sorry I'm so late. I'm glad to be here. It's been a long day. I'll have [a/some beer], please. Just milk, please. |

E Progress check

Complete the sentences with the most suitable alternative. Sometimes more than one answer is correct.

1 This is _____ busy time of year!

   a such
   b so
   c such a

2 Hello, _____ John Bradshaw speaking.

   a here is
   b it's
   c this is

3 Do you know how I can _____ with him?

   a get in touch
   b get hold
   c contact

4 We've hired _____ new workers.

   a much
   b several
   c a lot

5 She is _____ another line at the moment.

   a at
   b on
   c with

6 I work in _____ Purchasing Department of a large engineering company.

   a a
   b the
   c –

7 The meeting is _____ next month.

   a in
   b on
   c –

8 I've been trying _____ you.

   a contact
   b contacting
   c to contact

9 I'm a bit tied _____ at the moment.

   a up
   b down
   c –

10 We could meet the day _____ tomorrow.

   a before
   b after
   c following

11 Would you mind _____ her that I called?

   a tell
   b to tell
   c telling

12 She is very friendly, but she can be _____ when necessary.

   a outgoing
   b reliable
   c tough

13 We open at 4 am your time. We are five hours _____ you.

   a ahead of
   b behind
   c after

14 _____ me get him to call you in the morning.

   a Let
   b Shall
   c Would you like

15 Could you _____ him to call me back?

   a say
   b tell
   c ask

16 I have very _____ contacts in the construction business.

   a few
   b little
   c good

17 – What can I get you?
   – I'll have _____ beer, please.

   a a
   b some
   c the

18 I never have _____ problems with my English.

   a some
   b any
   c the

COMPANIES

A Introduction

1 CONTENTS

2 REVISION

1 How many company job titles can you name in one minute?

e.g. chief accountant, technical director, assistant purchasing manager, etc.

2 Revise the names of industries.

Which industries do your friends and/or relatives work in?
How many service industries can you name (e.g. banking, advertising, etc.)?
How many manufacturing industries can you name (e.g. the car industry, the building industry, etc.)?

3 Revise the Present Simple and Present Continuous tenses. Underline the correct forms of the verb. Then write two more examples of each tense.

e.g. I live / am living in Vancouver.

a Everyone works / is working overtime at the moment.
b Nobody ever goes / is going home before five o'clock.
c She shows / is showing some customers round the factory.
d Two and two make / are making four.

4 Write the comparative and superlative forms of these adjectives. Then use them in sentences.

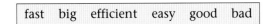

| fast big efficient easy good bad |

e.g. This system is faster than that one.
       Which system is the fastest?

5 Revise prepositions of place and direction. Give directions to the place where you work. Describe the internal layout.

6 Revise I (don't) think/believe... and In my opinion/view... . What is your opinion of the following?

• taking home work in the evenings;
• husbands and wives working for the same company;
• commuting to your workplace;
• living in the town/country.

B Your company

1 ACTIVITY

Company background
information

1 Work with a partner. Find out about the organisation which he/she
works for, using the following headings.

- type of company
- main products or activities
- number of employees
- annual turnover
- profitability
- main markets
- location of parent company
- location of offices, plants, etc.

2 How does this organisation chart compare with yours? Describe the
organisation of your company to a partner.

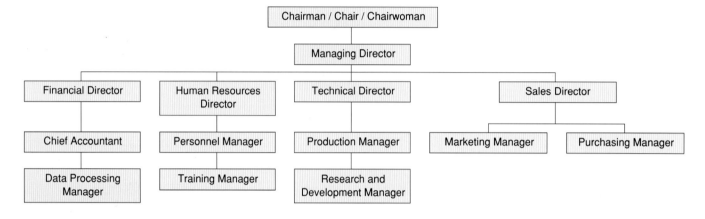

3 Find out the location of your partner's company. Where is it? How do
you get there?

Useful language

in the north of [the country]
south of [the river]
on the coast
to the west of [the town]
not far from [Berlin]
about 50 kilometres north-east of [Recife]
(right) in the centre of town
on/off [the ringroad]
just outside a village called [Hinton]

4 Describe the layout of your company.

Useful language

over there
across [the yard]
(on) the other side of [that building]
to the left/right of
on the [second] floor
at the top/bottom of the stairs
at the end of the corridor
the [third] door on the left/right

▲ 'It's just on the other side of that
building there.'

2 LANGUAGE POINTS

Revise high numbers (see page
98).

1 In how many ways can you say these figures?

a $0.25m
b £1.25m
c DM 0.5m
d ¥3.5m
e FFr 0.75bn
f Ptas 3.75bn

Some general business
vocabulary

2 Complete the sentences with words from the box in the singular or plural form.

> subsidiary   client   acquisition   activity
> turnover ✓   employee   supplier   profit   sale

e.g. Our annual <u>turnover</u> is £3.5m.

a We have 500 _____ in our London plant.
b Our main _____ are in manufacturing.
c Last year, we made £$^1/_2$ m _____ .
d We made an important _____ in Australia last year.
e We now have _____ in ten countries.
f We try to keep our _____ happy by offering a good service.
g We insist that all of our _____ are registered for ISO 9000.
h _____ are better than they have ever been.

3 LISTENING

1 Look at the 'Pharos Single market adviser' form. What questions would you ask to obtain the necessary information?
2 Listen to the recording and fill in the form.
3 Fill in the copy of the form on page 138 for your company.

Complete and
return to:
The Manager,
Commercial
Banking Services,
National
Westminster Bank,
FREEPOST
Hounslow
TW4 5BR.

This information is
requested to
ensure that future
PHAROS
developments
accurately reflect
the needs of those
using the system.
It will not be used
for any unrelated
mailing activity
and will remain
absolutely
confidential.

_____
For internal use only
☐☐☐☐☐
_____

1 Name
Title   First Name   Surname

Position
Business Name
Business Address

Postcode
Telephone Number

2 Type of Business
Sole Proprietor ☐   PLC ☐
Partnership ☐   Subsidiary ☐
Private Limited Company ☐   Other ☐

3 Turnover
Up to £250,000 ☐   £1m-£5m ☐
£250,000-£1m ☐   £5m+ ☐

4 Currently involved in import/export
Export only ☐   Import and export ☐
Import only ☐   None ☐

5 Number of companies/divisions
1-2 ☐   3-6 ☐   6+ ☐

6 Number of employees
1-9 ☐   31-100 ☐
10-30 ☐   100+ ☐

7 Is your company
NatWest Customer ☐   Member of CBI ☐
Emst & Young Client ☐   Other ☐

8 Please indicate your company's main business activities
Agriculture, forestry and fishing ☐
Energy and water supply ☐
Mining, chemicals ☐
Metal goods, engineering, vehicles ☐
Electronics ☐
Other manufacturing industries ☐
Construction ☐
Retail, distribution, hotels, catering, repairs ☐
Transport, communications ☐
Banking, financial, business services ☐
Education, health, government and local authorities ☐
Other ☐

9 Bankers
NatWest ☐   Barclays ☐   Midland ☐
Lloyds ☐   RBS ☐   Other ☐

10 Disk size required
3½" ☐   5¼" ☐

Copyright in PHAROS is the joint property of National Westminster Bank PLC and Emst and Young.
You will be licensed to use PHAROS on a single computer only for your internal business purposes, but not for the provision of information or advice to third parties. PHAROS may not be copied, save for any transient copies necessarily created by using PHAROS. You may not modify, de-compile or disassemble PHAROS.
PHAROS is supplied "as is" without warranties of any kind. PHAROS is intended as general guidance only. On any specific matter reference should be made to an appropriate professional adviser.

Signature _____
                              Date _____

C A company profile

◀ A 400,000
kilovolt line
in Brittany,
France

PHOTOTHEQUE EDF/MARC MORCEAU

PHOTOTHEQUE EDF/MICHEL BRIGAUD

1 READING

Promotional material

What is EDF?

A law passed on April 8th 1946 created Electricité de France (EDF) as a state company. Most of the electricity production and distribution companies that existed in France at that time were nationalised. The same law gave EDF a monopoly over the transmission, distribution, import and export of electricity.

However, the law allowed other companies to own and exploit production units to cover their own electricity needs, provided they sold excess production exclusively to EDF.

Thus, EDF buys in some of its production from other electricity producers. In 1991, EDF production accounted for 94% of the electricity produced in France, whereas sales accounted for 97% of French electricity consumption. Today, EDF is the world's largest producer of cheap electricity.

1 Read the text. What is EDF's position in the French market?
2 Find phrases in the text which have a similar meaning to the following.

a brought into state ownership
b make use of
c facilities
d represented

2 LISTENING

Describing a public utility
company (see page 99)

Like and *as* (see page 99)

1 Listen to the interview with a representative of Electricité de France as she gives an overview of the company. What is her job? Tick the categories below that she discusses.

2 Make notes on your company using the categories below to help you. Then write a short profile. See page 99 for a sample based on EDF.

Type of company	[ ]	Market position	[ ]	Main site(s)	[ ]
History	[ ]	Customer base	[ ]	Turnover	[ ]
Main activities	[ ]	No. of employees	[ ]	Profit	[ ]

3 LANGUAGE POINTS

Make and *do*

1 Complete these phrases with *make* or *do*. Then use them in sentences.

a _____ a decision (on)
b _____ very well (with)
c _____ a lot of work (for)
d _____ plans
e _____ better/worse (than)
f _____ money / a profit
g _____ business (with)
h _____ notes (on)
i _____ some typing/filing
j _____ a point (about)
k _____ something/nothing (about)
l _____ an effort (to)

The Simple Present v. the Present Continuous (see page 99)

2 Write the verbs in the simple or continuous form.

e.g. The company <u>manufactures</u> (*manufacture*) components for the car industry.

a I _____ (*forget*) the name of the managing director.
b It _____ (*have*) a turnover of $10m.
c It _____ (*suffer*) from the effects of the recession.
d It _____ (*make*) a loss.
e What _____ (*you*) (*do*) with the photocopier?
f I _____ (*try*) to mend it.
g If our clients _____ (*consider*) moving, we _____ (*provide*) assistance.
h If companies _____ (*think*) of relocating, we _____ (*give*) advice.

Verbs normally used in the simple form

3 Note the simple form of the verbs below. Complete the sentences.

e.g. I hear <u>that EDF are opening a new power plant.</u>

a I believe _____ .
b We don't own _____ .
c I (can) hear _____ .
d I (can) smell _____ .
e I think I know _____ .
f I know _____ .
g I feel _____ .
h That _____ belongs to me.
i We are _____ , which means that _____ .

4 ACTIVITY

A brief profile

Work in pairs. Find out about your partner's company, and write a brief profile of it.

Useful language
What kind of company do you work for? When was your company founded? What are your main activities/customers/competitors? Where are you based? How many people work for the company? Tell me something about…

D Competitors

1 READING

1 Read the text. What is the main purpose of the press release?

> **PRESS RELEASE**.
> **Not to be released until 10 am, 13th March.**
>
> A new laminating line has been completed at A & B Laminator's factory in Arls. This £1.5m investment makes the A & B factory the most technologically advanced in Europe, and guarantees continued production at the factory employing 120 people.
>
> The new line increases the factory's annual production capacity to 20,000 tonnes of laminated material.
>
> A & B Laminators' annual turnover is approximately £8m. The Managing Director is Mr Bertrand Rosen and the Chairman of the Board of Directors is Mr Harry Roux.
>
> The Arls factory has a history of more than forty years of laminating various materials. In 1989, the factory became a subsidiary of the Japanese AMP Corporation. AMP is a diversified company with major interests in shipping, machinery and construction. Last year, its annual turnover was nearly £500m.
>
> In his speech at the opening ceremony, Mr Sei Iwamura emphasised that A & B Laminators is an excellent example of the collaboration between Japanese 'know-how' and local skills, and demonstrates how different

2 Find words in the text which have the same meaning as:

expertise	which employs	shares or investment	stressed
ensures	raises	sales	co-operation

2 LANGUAGE POINTS

> Revise (see page 100):
> i the comparative and superlative forms of adjectives;
> ii *less* and *least* in comparisons.

1 Answer the questions. Work in pairs.

a Can you think of a company which is smaller than yours?
b ...and one that has a higher turnover?
c Can you think of any jobs which would be more interesting than yours?
d ...and any which would be less interesting?
e Is job satisfaction more or less important than job security?
f What is the most enjoyable meal you have ever had?
g ...and the least enjoyable?

2 Read the statements. Number the companies in order of size, from [1] to [6].

Company A is by far the biggest.	[1]
Company B is about the same size as Company C.	[ ]
Company C is slightly bigger than Company B.	[ ]
Company D is a little smaller than Company B.	[ ]
Company E is the smallest company.	[ ]
Company F is far bigger than Company E, but smaller than all of the other companies.	[ ]

> Geographical areas

3 Give the names of countries in these areas.

a Eastern Europe _____
b Latin America _____
c The Far East _____
d North Africa _____
e The Middle East _____
f Central America _____
g The Pacific rim _____

Expressing opinions

4 In pairs, compare what you think about:

- protectionist policies;
- privatisation;
- management buyouts;

- working overtime;
- segregated staff dining-rooms;
- company cars and other perks.

Useful language	
What do you think?	I (don't) think/believe...
What's your opinion?	I (don't) consider that...
Do you agree with me?	In my opinion/view...
You agree with me, don't you?	I'm (not) convinced that...

3 ACTIVITY

Comparing companies

▲ 'How does your turnover compare with A & B's?'

Omega Laminating Ltd have recently opened a new factory. Study the details below. Then, in pairs, compare Omega with the company featured in the press release opposite.

e.g. A & B have a far greater production capacity.
     Omega are probably more specialised.

> ### Notes on Omega Laminating Ltd
>
> New factory opened in Backtown, June 1993
> Company owned by the Fordex family
> 2 laminating lines
> Investment cost: £2.5m
> 100 people employed
> Annual production capacity – 15,000 tonnes of laminated material per year
> Annual turnover to June – £5m
>
> Background: The Fordex family has operated a factory in Backtown for over a hundred years. They are specialists in laminating and this factory replaces their old factory which was destroyed by a fire two years ago.

Useful language
How does the [investment cost] compare?
What about [turnover]?
What are the [production] figures?
Do you know who owns the companies?
Do you know anything about the history of the companies?

4 LISTENING

Talking about the competition

Match the phrases which best describe the competition faced by the following companies.

a A toy manufacturer
b A mining company
c A machinery manufacturer
d A firm of solicitors
e A construction company

i Competition coming from S.E.Asia
ii No competition
iii Hard competition
iv Facing hard price competition
v Almost no competition at the moment

Answers and key phrases, page 100

E Progress check

Complete the sentences with the most suitable alternative. Sometimes more than one answer is correct.

1 Ted _____ sales co-ordination.

   a is responsible for
   b is head of
   c leads

2 Their prices are _____ than ours.

   a the less competitive
   b less competitive
   c the least competitive

3 What _____ on at the moment?

   a do you work
   b are you working
   c are you doing

4 I report to the _____ manager.

   a personnel
   b personal
   c human resources

5 I need to check with our _____ department.

   a law
   b legislation
   c legal

6 _____ the whole building?

   a Do you own
   b Are you owning
   c Don't you own

7 Investment costs were _____ ever.

   a higher
   b highest
   c the highest

8 Our annual turnover is _____ .

   a two point five million
   b two and a half million
   c two million and a half

9 The quality of our products is _____ higher.

   a far
   b much
   c very

10 We are _____ a lot of progress.

   a going
   b doing
   c making

11 My office is _____ that building.

   a on the outskirts of
   b at the bottom of
   c on the other side of

12 I _____ we _____ compete with them.

   a think... can't
   b don't think... can
   c really don't think... can

13 _____ better today?

   a Do you feel
   b Are you feeling
   c How are you feeling

14 The training department is in _____ .

   a that door
   b the basement
   c the third floor

15 We face _____ competition from South-East Asia.

   a bad
   b hard
   c tough

16 I trained _____ a project manager when I was working in Canada.

   a like
   b as
   c –

17 We specialise _____ looms for the textile industry.

   a to produce
   b on producing
   c in producing

18 Our local power company is _____ .

   a ...a government company.
   b ...state-owned.
   c ...publicly owned.

PERSONNEL

A Introduction

1 CONTENTS

2 REVISION

1 Revise vocabulary used to describe people. Then describe someone you work with (or someone with you now). Refer to their height, age, hair, face, eyes and clothing.

2 Revise the language used to talk about family relationships. Then tell a partner about your family.

Are you married/single?
Do you have any children?
What does your [sister-in-law] do?
Are your parents retired?
How is everyone in your family? Are they all well?

3 Revise the Past Simple and Past Continuous tenses. Say what you did or what you were doing last Monday and/or Tuesday at these times.

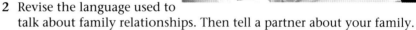

| 8.00 | 10.00 | 12.00 | 14.00 | 17.00 | 21.00 |

e.g. I got up at 8 am last Monday.
    I was working in my office at ten o'clock.

4 Revise the Present Perfect tense. Talk about your day so far.

Have you checked your mail?
        made any calls?
        had any visitors?
        attended any meetings?

5 Write down as many countries and nationalities as you can in two minutes. Talk about the nationality of people you have worked with.

e.g. Brazil → Brazilian
    Japan → Japanese
    Germany → German

6 Name:

a the rooms in a home;
b the internal areas of a place of work.

e.g. kitchen, spare bedroom, etc.
    boardroom, corridor, etc.

B Personal background

1 ACTIVITY

| Personal background |

Write questions using the prompts. Then ask a partner about him/herself.

where – born? *Where were you born?*
still – live – there? _____
where – live – now? _____
house – flat? _____
married? _____
children? _____
boys – girls? _____
ages? _____
where – go – school, college, university, etc.? _____
what – do – free time? _____

2 LISTENING

| Personal news
Still and *yet* |

1 Note these examples of *still* and *yet*.

  Are you still working for...?
  I still work in the same office.
  Is the work ready yet?
  You can't go yet!

2 Two men meet by chance and exchange news. Listen to the recording and underline the words in the boxes which relate to the main speaker. Do they know each other well?

3 Working in pairs, practise exchanging personal news. Use the vocabulary in the boxes as necessary.

Work

clerical/manual worker
director, manager, sales executive
self-employed, unemployed
retired, made redundant
full-time/part-time employment

Interests

collecting antiques/coins
playing cards/football
reading, watching TV
skiing, boating, walking
cookery, gardening, DIY
theatre, cinema, concerts

Health

back pain, arthritis
asthma, hayfever
sinus/heart trouble
(migraine) headaches

Accommodation

a detached/semi-detached/terraced house
a flat, a maisonette, a bungalow

3 LANGUAGE POINT

| Revise the Present Perfect tense
(see page 101). |

1 Read the sentences and write one more of each. Use the prompts if necessary.

a Have you ever worked in advertising?
  (ever play) _____
b How long have you worked for CAB TV?
  (live) _____
c Output has increased this year.
  (fall) _____
d The Chairman has resigned.
  (retire) _____
e I have just seen your ex-boss.
  (just meet) _____
f They haven't replied yet.
  (call yet) _____
g I still haven't decided.
  (still make his mind up) _____

▲ 'Have they arrived at a decision yet?'

4 READING

Revise *have to* and *had to* (see page 102).

2 In pairs, practise using the Present Perfect tense. Talk about:

Experiences
e.g. – Have you ever worked in...?
     – No, never. / Yes, (a long time ago).

The unfinished past
e.g. – How long have you been here?
     – Since June. / For two years.

Developments
e.g. – We've expanded greatly in the last year.
     – Yes, I know. / That's good.

News
e.g. – TLK have closed down.
     – Really? When did that happen?

Current information
e.g. – I haven't completed my report yet.
     – Why's that? / When do you think you will?

1 Read the advertisement. What do you think it is selling?
2 Match the questions in the text with the responses below.

Have you...

Ever had to catch the 7 am shuttle?

Ever had to m-m-make a speech?

Ever been stuck in a suit when it's 80° in the shade?

Ever been stuck in Stuttgart?

Ever had to sit through a sales conference?

Ever had to be nice to a smart-ass?

Ever had to fire someone?

Ever been misquoted by a trade journalist?

Ever had to cancel a holiday?

Ever had to have 'one last drink' with a client?

Ever worked so late you've slept in the office?

Ever missed the last shuttle home?

Ever wondered why you put yourself through all this?

Because you're a professional. That's why.

CLERICAL MEDICAL

THE CHOICE OF THE PROFESSIONAL

---

a When do you expect the fog to clear?
b What time is the first flight in the morning?
c What time is lunch?
d That's very, very interesting.
e Something unexpected has come up.
f OK, but then I really must go...
g Ladies and gentlemen...
h Is that really the time?
i Is it always as hot as this?
j I hate getting up early in the morning.
k I'm sorry to have to tell you...
l I'm sure I didn't say that.

C Conditions of work

1 READING

Office equipment and furniture

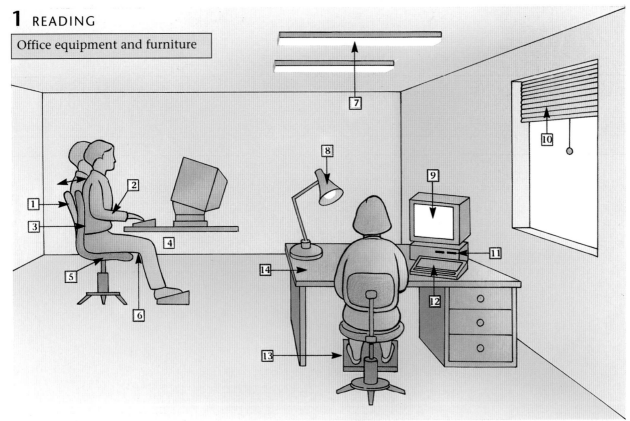

1 Match these captions with the numbered boxes in the diagram.

a Adequate lighting
b Table lamp: not too bright, no glare or distracting reflections
c Forearms approximately horizontal
d Adjustable seat back
e Screen: stable image, adjustable, readable, glare- and reflection-free
f Good back support
g Window covering
h Adjustable seat height
i Leg room: enough space to allow user to change position
j No excess pressure on backs of thighs and backs of knees
k Work surface: spacious, glare-free, allowing flexible arrangements
l Software: appropriate to task, adapted to user
m Keyboard: usable, adjustable, detachable, legible
n Foot support if needed

Too/Enough + to/for (page 103)

2 In pairs, discuss your working environment.

e.g. Is it comfortable to work in?
      Is there enough space for everyone?
      Is it quiet enough (for you to be able to concentrate)?
      Is the lighting bright enough (for you not to strain your eyes)?

2 LANGUAGE POINT

The Past Perfect tense: *I had already left the company when...* (see page 103).

Put the verbs in brackets into either the Simple Past (*did*) or the Past Perfect tense (*had done*).

a I _____ (*ask*) Maria Sanchez to join us for dinner yesterday.
b Unfortunately, she _____ (*arrange*) to be somewhere else.
c She _____ (*call*) me last night.
d She said she _____ (*try*) to change her arrangements...
e ...but it _____ (*not be*) possible.

f   She _____ (*not know*) you were coming.
g   She _____ (*want*) to meet you very much.
h   I tried to call you, but you _____ (*leave*) the office.

3 LISTENING

Revise the Past Continuous tense: *I was talking to a client when...* (see page 103).

1   Put questions from the table to a partner. Write down his/her replies.

Where were you living	this time last year/month?
Where were you working	on Tuesday morning?
What were you doing	at 2 pm on Friday?
What were you working on	between three and four yesterday?

2   Listen to the following people talking about a fire in their office. Tick the ones who were still in the building. What were they all doing at the time?

Sofia Fallon   [ ]   _____
Sheila Kite   [ ]   _____
Andrew Syrah   [ ]   _____
Steven Upton   [ ]   _____

4 ACTIVITY

Talking about fringe benefits

WHO GETS THE PERKS

Job title	Average basic salary	Bonus scheme	Employer's pension contribution	Private health insurance	Company car	Home telephone bill paid	Life assurance cover – × salary
Director / Managing director	£45,000	£10,000			Yes (90%)	Yes	4×
Senior manager / Chief accountant			£2,425	Employee and family			
Middle manager / Production manager	£16,900	£1,025			Possible (26%)		3×
Senior secretary			£975	No		No	
Skilled operative / Craftsman	£10,625	£1,675			No		2×

In pairs, complete the chart.

Partner A: Your information is above.
Partner B: Your information is on page 103.

Useful language

What is a [managing director's] basic salary?
Does he or she get private health insurance?
What does it cover?
Does the company pay his/her phone bill?
Is there a bonus scheme?
What is it worth?

D Job descriptions

1 READING

1 Catherine Hicks is a 27 year old management consultant. What in you opinion, qualifies someone to be a management consultant?

2 Read the text about Catherine Hicks and answer the questions below.

Catherine Hicks is a qualified accountant and spends much of her time advising corporate clients and local and central government on how best to implement environmental management systems. 'Any company that is seriously committed to the environment should adopt management systems which combine consideration for the environment with the day-to-day running of the company,' she argues.

Her principal interest, however, is in larger global issues. She has just completed a project, financed by the Overseas Development Administration, to reduce the levels of carbon dioxide in Zimbabwe. Before that, the consultancy carried out a study for the Ministry of Environment and Forests in India to assess the economic costs to the Indian Government of complying with the Montreal Protocol on

CFCs. Hicks is soon to embark on a similar project in Romania.

■ Background: read Geography at Oxford, graduating with a 2:1 in 1986. Qualified as a chartered accountant with Touche Ross in 1990 and has been in the environmental consultancy group for 18 months.
Hours: 45 hours a week
Salary: £27,000

Source: *The Daily Telegraph*, 20/2/92

a What kind of clients does Catherine Hicks mainly work with?
b What does she spend most of her time doing?
c What was her most recent job?
d Where is her next project?
e When did she leave university?

Talking about qualifications

3 Note the following expressions.

I studied law at [Michigan State University] for [two years].
I have a degree in [business studies] from [Universidade de Mackenzie].
I trained as a [chartered accountant] with [Touche Ross].
I qualified as a [quantity surveyor] with [MacAlpine] in [1981].
I am a qualified [actuary].

4 In pairs, discuss these questions.

a What qualifications have you got?
b What qualifications are required for your job?
c What qualifications were required for your last job?

2 LISTENING

Talking about the job you do

Sonya Reed talks about what it is like to work for a manufacturing company based in the south of England. Answer the questions.

a What is her present job?
b What does the job involve?
c When does she have dealings with the factory floor?
d How does she feel about her lack of contact with the shop floor?
e How long has she been with the company?
f Has she always had the same job?
g What does she do in her free time?
h Does she spend much time with her colleagues outside working hours?

3 LANGUAGE POINTS

> Replying to negative sentences
> (see page 104):
> – So it's not far away?
> – No, (it isn't).

1 In pairs, practise confirming negative sentences.

e.g. So you aren't responsible for [petty cash]?   No, I'm not.

a You don't speak [Spanish], (do you?)   _____
b They haven't finished yet, (have they?)   _____
c So you can't make the meeting.   _____
d They didn't phone, (did they?)   _____
e You wouldn't do that, (would you?)   _____

> Physical descriptions:
> appearance and dress (see page 104)

2 Look at the photograph of Tracy Wyman. Mark the notes true [T], false [F], don't know [?].

3 Write notes on Jonathan Dean.

▲ Tracy Wyman

▲ Jonathan Dean

Tracy Wyman -
quite tall, slim
has straight blond hair
is wearing a short skirt
a silk blouse
woolly tights
high-heeled shoes

> Adjectives and their opposites
> (see page 105)

4 Write the opposites to these adjectives. In pairs, discuss which can be applied to people, which to a job, and which to a written report.

interesting	uninteresting	efficient	_____
quiet	_____	reliable	_____
dishonest	_____	disappointing	_____
generous	_____	intolerant	_____
pleasant	_____	intelligent	_____
thoughtless	_____	polite	_____
good-looking	_____	thorough	_____
hard-working	_____	organised	_____

4 ACTIVITY

> Making recommendations, suggestions and criticisms
> *Wish* (see page 105)

1 Note these common phrases.

Can/Could I make a suggestion?   You should...
I wish you would...   Have you thought of [wearing a tie]?
Why don't you...?

2 Note these common expressions.

I don't think you should...   I wish you wouldn't...
It's not a good idea to...   You shouldn't...

3 Work in pairs.
Partner A: You are Tracy or Jonathan.
Partner B: You are Tracy or Jonathan's boss. Criticise their clothes and suggest others...

a ...for reorganising a storeroom.
b ...for taking clients to a dinner dance.
c ...for a trip to the coast.

e.g. I don't think you should wear a suit. Why don't you wear an overall?

E Progress check

Complete the sentences with the most suitable alternative. Sometimes more than one answer is correct.

1 I occasionally wear a _____-striped suit to work.

   a line
   b pin
   c vertical

2 I was made _____ in June.

   a retired
   b unemployed
   c redundant

3 _____ ready yet?

   a The work is
   b Is the work
   c The work isn't

4 There isn't enough room in the warehouse _____ this delivery.

   a for
   b to
   c to store

5 Catherine Hicks is qualified _____ .

   a accountant
   b in accountancy
   c as an accountant

6 How long have you _____ ?

   a married
   b been married
   c had a marriage

7 So you haven't finished yet?

   a No, I haven't.
   b Yes, I haven't.
   c Yes, I have.

8 Is there _____ space to work in?

   a adequate
   b plenty
   c enough

9 She has a _____ in her back.

   a pain
   b problem
   c trouble

10 She _____ for her previous employer for five years.

   a has worked
   b worked
   c had worked

11 Sean Klein _____ a degree in French and German.

   a made
   b studied
   c did

12 _____ in the manufacturing industry before she joined this company?

   a Has she worked
   b Had she worked
   c Did she work

13 _____ ever had to make a speech?

   a Do you
   b Did you
   c Have you

14 I wish he _____ wear that jacket in the office.

   a won't
   b wouldn't
   c doesn't

15 It's too hot in my office _____ properly.

   a to work
   b for working
   c for work

16 _____ for NHK?

   a Do you still work
   b Do you work still
   c Are you still working

17 Sonya Reed is secretary _____ the production director.

   a for
   b with
   c to

18 I was in a meeting. When I heard the alarm, I _____ the building.

   a was leaving
   b left
   c had left

A Introduction

PRODUCTS

1 CONTENTS

A Introduction
B The products you make/use
C Product descriptions
D Compliments and complaints
E Progress check

2 REVISION

1 Revise numbers and symbols. Can you say the following? Write four more examples and say them.

1,250   1.25 $150   12/4/93   1³/₄   12.5%   £125,000   1/12/62

2 Revise weights and measurements. Can you say the following? Write four more examples and say them.

15gm   175lbs   5m × 8m   2.5cm   100kph   21°C

3 Put these materials into sets. Then discuss objects around you.

wood   plastic   glass   steel   paper   polystyrene
cotton   nylon   rubber   silver   leather   wool

metal _____
man-made _____
natural _____

e.g. – What's this made of?
   – It's made of wood.

4 Revise the Present Perfect Simple tense and the Simple Past tense. Then put the verbs in brackets into the appropriate tense.

a What time _____ (*you, call*) me this morning?
b _____ (*you, call*) the factory yet?
c _____ (*you, call*) me yesterday?
d I _____ (*be*) in Scotland then.
e _____ (*you, ever, be*) to Scotland?

5 Revise the order of adjectives. Then use two adjectives from the box with each of the following nouns.

big   cold   expensive   French   grey   hot   interesting
metal   nice   old   wonderful   wooden   new   sunny

car _____   box _____
chair _____   film _____
drink _____   day _____

6 Revise relative pronouns. Tick the correct sentences.

a The company who we are talking about is...   [ ]
b The people which we are training are...   [ ]
c The organisation we are joining is...   [ ]
d The prices that we are charging are...   [ ]
e The products which we are launching are...   [ ]

B The products you make/use

1 LISTENING

Adverbs in phrases: *highly competitive, reasonably priced,* etc. (see page 107)

1 Match the products with the key selling points.
2 Make similar statements about your products.

a Industrial clothing   i   Stylish and very economical
b Educational toys   ii   Highly competitive prices and very durable
c Furniture and fittings   iii   Quality, price, original designs
d Glass conservatories   iv   Extremely well-made, three-month guarantee

2 LANGUAGE POINTS

Numbers and symbols (see page 107)

Materials and substances (see page 107)

1 Can you say the following?

a 12/4734-AZ97   c $^3/_8$ e 14 sq m   g 25% = $^1/_4$
b 17-VLD/44/900   d $^1/_{10}$ f 37 cu cm   h 66.6% = $^2/_3$

2 Name two materials or substances that might be used in the production of the following items.

a a desk   c a bridge   e a suit   g a cello
b a VDU   d a wall   f a suitcase   h a sandwich

3 READING AND LISTENING

Making a product enquiry

1 Read the exchange of letters, and answer the questions opposite. What is the sales manager's response to the inquiry?

SM Electrics

67, Dune Heights, Woollamoora, NSW Australia
Tel: 39 41 521   Fax: 39 42 670

The Sales Manager   Ref 12/AS/DB
RA Plastics   June 1st, 19..
56 Marino Road
Singapore 0923
Republic of Singapore

Dear Sir/Madam,

We are a major manufacturer of electrical goods for the Australian market, and we are currently reviewing our list of suppliers of components. Your company has been recommended to us by RG Holdsworth as a reliable producer of plastic casings.

We would be very grateful if you could forward details of your range of products, together with price lists and delivery charges.

We look forward to hearing from you by June 20th at which time we shall be finalising our plans to visit prospective suppliers in the ASEAN area.

Yours faithfully,

Andrea P Soleman

Andrea Soleman
Chief Buyer

RA PLASTICS

56 Marino Road
Singapore 0923
Republic of Singapore
Tel: 33 64 119
Fax: 33 64 129

Your ref 12/AS/DB
June 14th, 19..

Ms Andrea Soleman
SM Electrics
67, Dune Heights
Woollamoora
NSW Australia

Dear Ms Soleman,

Thank you for your letter of June 1st. I enclose details of our product range, price lists and delivery terms, as requested.

We were extremely interested in your enquiry and we very much hope that you will be able to visit us in Singapore. I am sure that there are many areas in which we can co-operate.

Please contact us as soon as you know your itinerary.

Yours sincerely,

Tony Pang Wan

Tony Pang Wan
Sales Manager

a What is the main market of SM Electrics?
b Who recommended RA Plastics?
c What information does Andrea Soleman need?
d Why does she need it by June 20th?

2 Listen to the telephone call between Tony Pang Wan and Andrea Soleman. What arrangement do they make to meet?

A follow-up phone call

4 ACTIVITY

Ordering products
Used to (see page 107)

Work in pairs.

Partner A: Your information is below. You wish to order 20 of each of these wall clocks, but you only have an old copy of the brochure.

Partner B: Your information is on page 106, and it comes from the current edition of the brochure.

Useful language
I would like to order... Do you still stock...? You used to supply... What is the nearest equivalent?

Solid brass frame, white dial, quartz movement.
Diameter: 240mm (9½″)
Catalogue no: A444-908
£54

Battery-operated round quartz wall clock. Red case with easy-to-read graphics and non-scratch glass.
Diameter: 229mm (9″)
Catalogue no: A490-89
£25

£35
Quartz movement, black frame, silver dial.
Diameter: 240mm (9½″)
Catalogue no: A444-911

C Product descriptions

1 READING

Imperial measurements (see page 108)

Read the product information from a publicity brochure. Then answer the questions below. Does the text give the company's main market?

THE BIGGEST NAME IN BIG BALLOONS

Cameron is the largest manufacturer of hot-air balloons in the world. On average, we build one balloon every day, and Cameron factories in the United Kingdom, United States, Australia and Russia account for more than 40% of annual global balloon sales – you'll find our products flying in at least 50 countries. We've been making balloons for over 20 years – no other manufacturer can match our experience or our expertise.

The Viva series

The Cameron Viva provides the most inexpensive combination of strength and performance available in any hot-air balloon.

Ranging in size from a single-seat air-chair of 20,000 cubic feet (590 cu m) to a five-person 90,000 cubic feet (2550 cu m) envelope, the seven Viva models are particularly suitable for sport ballooning.

All envelope colour and basket trim options are available to customise your Viva, and for entry into ballooning at the lowest possible cost, ask about the off-the-shelf Viva Packages.

Mark these statements true [T], false [F], or don't know [?].

a No other manufacturer has as much experience as Cameron.   [ ]
b Cameron has been making balloons since 1979.   [ ]
c Cameron's market share is 40%.   [ ]
d Cameron builds balloons in more than 50 countries.   [ ]
e The Viva is the cheapest hot-air balloon on the market.   [ ]
f The Viva range comes in seven different models.   [ ]
g Viva balloons are usually made to order.   [ ]

2 LANGUAGE POINTS

The Present Perfect Continuous tense (see page 108)

1 Note these examples.

I have been talking to the people at GHQ.
She has been working for ABP since June.
How long have you been learning English?
Have you been waiting long?

2 Put one verb in the Present Perfect Simple and the other in the Continuous.

a He _____ (*never meet*) the MD.
  He _____ (*work*) for the company for 11 years.
b They _____ (*make*) hang-gliders since 1984.
  They _____ (*produce*) over 3000 hang-gliders in that time.

c I _____ (*call*) clients all morning.
   I _____ (*only speak*) to five so far.
d It _____ (*rain*) three times this week.
   It _____ (*rain*) all day today.

Indirect questions (see page 108)

3 Write an indirect form of these questions, using *Do you know...?*, *I'd like to know...*, *Can you tell me...*, etc.

e.g. What does it look like?
      <u>Could you tell me what it looks like?</u>

a How big is it?
   _____

b Does it run on petrol or gas?
   _____

c How often does it need servicing?
   _____

d Where can I buy it?
   _____

e Can you deliver it on Friday afternoon?
   _____

f How soon can you arrange delivery?
   _____

Shapes

4 Draw these shapes. Then work in pairs. Match the shapes to the objects. Can you give other examples?

a round
b square
c oval
d triangular
e rectangular
f heart-shaped
g L-shaped
h in the shape of a cross

a rugby ball
a cigarette packet
a wheel
a shield
a pyramid
a golf club
a plus sign
a chess board

▲ Cameron is the world market leader in special shape hot-air balloons.

3 LISTENING

Describing a production process

Revise the Simple Present Passive tense (see page 109).

Listen to someone describing how a balloon is made. Put these steps in the right order.

a At this stage in the construction, the envelope has a hole at the top.
b The nylon is cut into panels.
c Wires connect the envelope with the burner.
d The nylon panels are sewn together.

4 ACTIVITY

Prepare a short presentation. Describe:

a your product range;
b a particular product;
c how that product is made.

Useful language

First...
Then/Next...
After/Before that...
At this stage...
Finally...

D Compliments and complaints

1 READING

A notice of product recall

A letter of complaint (see page 110)

1 Read the product recall notice below, and answer the questions. Why has the notice been issued?

2 Working in pairs, write a letter of complaint to PX Alarms from a stockist who hasn't seen the product recall notice. There is a sample letter on page 110.

IMPORTANT SAFETY NOTICE

SMOKE ALARMS

As a responsible company, PX Alarms, a division of the PX group of companies, is recalling all of their XC-4 range of smoke alarms.

We have discovered a fault which may invalidate the working of a number of the alarms in this range.

To identify the alarm, please remove from the wall and check the code on the back of the casing; the code is clearly stamped on the back. Only the range coded XC-4 is affected. All other alarms are completely unaffected.

If you have an XC-4 alarm, please stop using it immediately and return it to us at the address below for testing. All postage and testing costs will be borne by PX Alarms.

The company would like to apologise for any inconvenience caused.

Mark the statements true [T], false [F] or don't know [?].

a All XC-4 models are faulty.   [ ]
b The XC-4 can be clearly identified.   [ ]
c The code number is visible on the front.   [ ]
d The cost of testing the faulty models will be high.   [ ]

2 ACTIVITY

Expressing satisfaction and dissatisfaction

1 Note these examples of compliments and responses.

Compliments

We were / have been very pleased with it.
It was / has been excellent.
It worked / has been working very well indeed.
We have not had any trouble with it since we've had it. / since we bought it.

◀▶

Responses

Yes, we are very pleased with it too.
We have had excellent feedback from our customers.
We have had a very good response from our clients.
That's good to hear.
Thank you for telling us.

2 Work in pairs.

Partner A praises Partner B's product.
Partner B responds.

◀ 'We have had excellent feedback from our customers.'

3   Note these examples of complaints and responses.

Complaints

> We'd/I'd like to make a complaint.
> We are very unhappy about...
> [Its performance] isn't good enough.
> [The noise it makes] is terrible.
> It has broken down [three times] since we bought it.

◀▶

Responses

> We are very sorry (about it).
> That is very unfortunate.
> I am very sorry to hear that.
> What can we do to put it right?

4   Work in pairs.

Partner B complains about **Partner A**'s product.
Partner A responds.

3 LISTENING

Causes for complaint

Need + -ing (*It needs mending.*)

Listen to the recording. What is wrong with the car? Choose from the phrases in the box.

> scratched   broken   dented   doesn't work
> loose   bent   leaking   stiff   cracked

paintwork _____
bumper _____
petrol tank _____
headlamp _____
windows _____
petrol gauge _____

4 LANGUAGE POINTS

Revise relative pronouns (see page 109)

1   Rewrite the examples using *who, which, whose,* etc.

a   This is the woman. Her car was damaged.
_____

b   The hotel is expensive. I stayed there.
_____

c   I wrote down the fax number. He gave it to me.
_____

d   Have you found that file? You lost it yesterday.
_____

e   I drove to Leoton. We have a warehouse there.
_____

f   The man is very helpful. He works in the office next to mine.
_____

g   I work for a Taiwanese company. It manufactures electronic toys.
_____

h   That's the man. It's his job to deal with these enquiries.
_____

Order of adjectives (see page 110)

2   Use adjectives from the box to describe the products below.

> answer   photocopying   tennis   smoke
> fibreglass   plastic   nylon   stainless steel
> French   German   Japanese   American   Italian
> green   black   grey   blue   cream
> square   new   cheap   faulty   efficient   light

racket   *a black fibreglass tennis racket* _____
phone _____
alarm _____
machine _____
desk _____

E Progress check

Complete the sentences with the most suitable alternative. Sometimes more than one answer is possible.

1 She's in Singapore. She _____ there for two months.

   a worked
   b has worked
   c has been working

2 I'd like to complain about this...

   a metal dented table lamp.
   b dented metal table lamp.
   c dented metal lamp table.

3 Our products are reasonably _____ .

   a cheap
   b priced
   c price

4 There are several faulty items that need _____ .

   a mending
   b to mend
   c to be mended

5 Do you know _____ servicing?

   a how often does it need
   b how often it needs
   c whether it needs

6 Did you speak to the customer _____ secretary made the complaint?

   a whose
   b who
   c that

7 It comes in a crate that is about _____ in size.

   a three cubic metres
   b three cubic feet
   c three square feet

8 The model number is 2A/70-Z.

   a 'two A stroke seven oh dash Z'
   b 'two A slash seven zero hyphen Z'
   c 'two A dash seven oh slash Z'

9 We are very sorry _____ that.

   a to hear
   b for
   c about

10 – Do you make them in other designs?
   – We _____ , but we don't any more.

   a use to
   b used to
   c used

11 Our conference tables are available in various shapes and sizes. That model is _____ .

   a round
   b in the shape of a circle
   c circle-shaped

12 We are _____ with it.

   a very pleased
   b pleased indeed
   c very pleased indeed

13 – How are they made?
   – _____ , the fabric is cut into squares.

   a First
   b At this stage
   c After that

14 Our profit margin is 33.1%, that's _____ .

   a about a third
   b more than a quarter
   c between a third and a half

15 – Your work is excellent.
   – Thank you _____ so.

   a for say
   b to say
   c for saying

16 We _____ them in that size.

   a make no longer
   b don't longer make
   c no longer make

17 They had terrible _____ from their customers.

   a complaints
   b information
   c feedback

18 – What is it _____ ?
   – The working parts are copper.

   a made of
   b made with
   c made by

A Introduction

1 CONTENTS

A Introduction
B The services you provide/use
C Dealing with problems
D Service companies
E Progress check

SERVICES

2 REVISION

1 How many service industries can you name? Can you name the ones you deal with?

2 Revise modal verbs: *could, should, ought to, need, may* and *might*. Write sentences that are true.

a I may/might _____ this week.
b I ought to _____ before the weekend.
c I should _____ , but I don't have time.
d I couldn't _____ , because _____ .
e We need to _____ because it's getting old.
f I would _____ , but _____ .

3 Revise *must/mustn't* and *have to/don't have to*. Use them to complete these sentences.

a _____ wear a company tie.
b _____ call my wife.
c _____ be late tomorrow.
d _____ drive on the right here.
e _____ meet for lunch some time.

4 Revise reflexive pronouns (*myself, yourself*, etc.). Then fill in the gaps.

a He thinks of _____ as someone special.
b I wasn't talking to _____ . I was dictating a memo!
c We had to tidy the room _____ .
d She paid for the ticket _____ .

5 Revise how to apologise and express regret. Mark the main stress in these sentences.

a I am sorry.   d I'm very sorry indeed.
b I'm so sorry.   e I'd like to apologise.
c I'm very sorry.   f Please accept my apologies.

6 Revise the expression *to have something done*. What jobs do you always do yourself? Which ones do you usually have done?

a at work
b outside work

B The services you provide/use

1 ACTIVITY

Lease and *purchase*

Payment times: *weekly*, *per week*, etc. (see page 111)

1 In pairs, say whether these items are bought or leased in your company. If leased, discuss the standard of service that you receive from the leasing company.

> telephone system   fax machines   buildings
>   photocopiers   computer systems   cars

2 **Partner A:** You work for an office equipment supplier. Your information is below.

Partner B: You are considering buying or leasing a fax machine. Your information is on page 111.

*G*et an F20 facsimile machine with nothing to pay for six months

* We offer a full maintenance service programme, costing £190 per annum, which incorporates a four working-hour response time, all spare parts, labour, travelling time, call outs (both routine and emergency) and all consumables, except paper.

* In addition, we include, free of charge, the facility to contact the Flash Centre, which can usually solve 80% of all problems over the phone.

All prices exclude VAT.

Lease over five years
£9.50 weekly

Lease over three years
£13.94 weekly

N.B. The first six months is free of charge.

Alternatively:

Outright Purchase Price	£1890.00
Less 20% discount	£378.00
Net invoice total	£1512.00

2 LISTENING

Talking about services

1 Listen and match the speakers with the right services. Is it a service they provide [P] or one they use [U]? Underline the reason for use.

Service	Speaker (a-d)	P/U	Reason for use
express parcel delivery	d		speed / insurance cover
emergency breakdown		P	good reputation / short waiting time
site maintenance			the cheapest option / a time-saving strategy
creche			friendly staff / good value

2 What services do you use? Why do you use them? Are they good value for money?

3 LANGUAGE POINTS

To have/get something done (see page 112)

Expressing necessity: *need, must,* etc. (see page 112)

Reflexive pronouns: *myself, ourselves,* etc.

Own

1 Expand the statements, using the verbs in the box.

> update   replace   service   paint   repair   clean ✓   change

e.g. The office carpet is very dirty.
(need) *We need to have it cleaned.*

a We've got some graffiti on the walls.
(must) _____

b One of the machines has broken down.
(have to) _____

c My car tyres are worn out.
(need) _____

d Our accounting system is very old-fashioned.
(ought to) _____

e The drum on my printer is getting old.
(must) _____

f We are having some problems with our fax machines.
(should) _____

2 Note the following examples.

I write my speeches myself.
I write my own speeches.   (NOT I write own speeches.*)

3 How many of these jobs do you and your colleagues do yourselves? How many do you have done for you?

photocopying	making coffee	office cleaning
posting letters	ordering taxis	car maintenance
sending faxes	redecorating house/flat	delivery of newspapers

◀ 'We're having a new network system put in at the moment.'

4 ACCENTS AND PRONUNCIATION

In-house arrangements v. subcontracting

Listen to the recording. Indicate whether the speakers' companies handle the services in-house [IH] or sub-contract them [SC].

	catering	security	cleaning	language training
A Senegalese technical programme officer				
A Chilean office clerk				
An Irish export manager				
A Dutch customer services manager				
A Scottish sales executive				

C Dealing with problems

1 READING

An exchange of letters

Due to, on account of, etc. (see page 112)

These letters make the situation worse. In pairs, identify where they go wrong and suggest changes.

Leadership Training Inc.

64 place d'Orsel, 93002 Paris
Tel. (1) 42 27 33688
Fax. (1) 42 27 37190
25 February 19..

Dear Ms Dill,

Leadership and Motivation Course, 2-3 March 19..

We regret that we have had to cancel this course due to an insufficient number of enrolments. The next Leadership and Motivation Course will be held on 2-3 June, and I have enrolled Mr Forest and Ms Sawcroft for these dates.

We apologise for any inconvenience which this might cause.

Yours sincerely,

Faith C. Vere

Faith Vere
Bookings Administrator

---

97 BELGRAVE CRESCENT, ABERDEEN 40C 9GL, SCOTLAND
TEL: 02761 309427; FAX: 02761 896 438

February 28th, 19..

Dear Ms Vere,

Leadership and Motivation Course, 2nd-3rd March 19..

I was very surprised to receive your letter of February 25th, and, I must admit, rather annoyed. You should have let us know sooner if you were planning to cancel the course. There was no indication in your course publicity that a course would be cancelled if there were not enough applicants. This fact should have been made clear in your advertising material.

I am also very unhappy about the way you have assumed that Mr Forest and Ms Sawcroft will attend your June course. In fact, these dates are not suitable for them.

I therefore ask you to cancel their places on this course and to refund the deposit which we have paid. I believe you have the number of our bank account.

Yours sincerely,

R. Dill

Rachel Dill
Group Training Co-ordinator

---

2 LANGUAGE POINTS

The Past tense of modal verbs (see page 113)

1 Respond to the statements.

e.g. Why didn't you tell us?
    (I should/tell/you) I should have told you.

a Where did you leave your papers?
   (I/must/leave/them/in the office) _____

▲ 'The money should have arrived by now.'

Apologising and accepting/
rejecting apologies (see page
113)

b Your line was engaged all day.
   (you/could/send/me/a fax) _____

c Why did you book me into that hotel?
   (you/should/check with me/first) _____

d Why did you need to call Linda?
   (she/might/forget/about/the meeting) _____

e We are disappointed with the way they handled it.
   (they/ought to/let us know) _____

f We have plenty of the items in stock.
   (we/need not/reordered/yet) _____

g There was no need to send a car for him.
   (he/could/walk) _____

h The call-out engineer made a mess of the repairs.
   (should/do/the job/ourselves) _____

2 Match the apologies with the responses.

a Sorry I'm so late. The traffic was terrible coming out of the airport.
b Sorry, I don't follow you.
c I do apologise for all the trouble we've caused.
d Excuse me, do you mind if I interrupt for a moment?
e I'd like to apologise for not coming to yesterday's meeting.

i   Of course not. Go ahead.
ii   Yes, it's a shame you couldn't come. You could have let us know.
iii Let me put it another way then.
iv   You should have called us from the airport. We were getting worried
     about you.
v   Don't worry. It's been no trouble. It really doesn't matter.

3 LISTENING

Sorting out a problem

A parcel has failed to arrive. Listen to the recording and answer the
questions.

a Which service did the customer use?
b What is the parcel reference number?
c When will Harriet West call back?
d What is the driver's story?
e What is Sandra Tempest's main concern?
f What action is she going to take?

4 ACTIVITY

Making and dealing with
complaints

Practise dealing with problems working in pairs.

Partner A: Complain. Accept or reject **Partner B**'s apologies. Accept or
reject **Partner B**'s proposed solutions.

Partner B: Express regret. Offer explanations. Propose alternatives
or solutions.

'You promised a twenty-four
hour call-out service. We've
been waiting for your
engineer for two days.'

Complaint 1

'You said that the money
would be transferred by the
end of the week. It still
hasn't arrived.'

Complaint 3

'You promised us next-day
delivery. That was two days
ago.'

Complaint 2

'You should have let us know
immediately. You obviously knew
that your stocks were running low.
We have had to stop one of our
machines because of this.'

Complaint 4

Answers and key phrases, page 112

D Service companies

1 ACTIVITY

Researching a catering business
Such as, etc. (see page 114)

▲ For special occasions, Sutcliffe provide the services of a butler.

Sutcliffe Catering West...

- operate more than 220 contracts in the South-West and South Wales, ranging in size from providing lunch for five, to complex operations for big employers such as British Gas South-West and Lloyds Bank for two or three thousand staff.

- serve 75,000 meals a day.

- is one of eight autonomous companies within a group with a combined turnover of more than £360 million a year.

Work in pairs.

Partner A: You are thinking of using Sutcliffe. After asking around, you have obtained the information on the left. Contact **Partner B**, who has used Sutcliffe before, and ask him/her about the following:

- number of employees;
- training policies;
- hygiene record;
- whether they advise on in-service catering facilities.

Partner B: Your information is on page 114.

2 LANGUAGE POINTS

Correcting misunderstandings

1 Using the information on Sutcliffe Catering, practise correcting misunderstandings. Work in pairs.

| They told me that...
 He/She said that...
 According to their sales people...
 Apparently... | | He/She can't/couldn't have said/meant...
 They must have said/meant...
 They wouldn't have said...
 You/I must have misunderstood... |

Jobs in service industries

2 Write jobs which go with these service industries.

law *solicitor, lawyer, judge* _____
insurance _____
bank _____
stock market _____
dentistry _____
medicine _____
hotel industry _____
police _____
fire service _____
information technology (IT) _____
security _____
catering _____

3 LISTENING

Fees and charges (see page 114)

1 In pairs, identify some people who would be paid commission, and some who would be paid a fee.

2 Match the speakers with the service industries.

a Peter Cox, warehouse manager
b Norman Gish, a private investor
c Donald Weston, a company secretary
d Vera Fredricks, an administration manager
e Zen Lombard, an office manager

i   insurance
ii   law firm
iii newspaper recycling
iv IT consultancy
v   stock broking

4 READING

A case of recycling

1 In pairs, answer these questions. What is a pallet? What is it made of? What is it used for?

2 Read the text and answer the questions below.

BRITISH COMPANY COLLECTS EMPTIES AND SAVES THOUSANDS

A British company is offering industry savings of thousands of pounds on the cost of pallets – the wooden platforms on which everything from cornflakes to computers is transported.

Up to now, companies have had two choices – to buy new pallets and see their stock diminish by theft, loss or damage, or to hire from a specialist company that collects and returns the empty pallets after use.

Hambrook Pallets, specialists in reconditioning, now offer user companies a third choice.

They supply reconditioned pallets to the factory, collect the empties, separate any that are damaged, and return them to Avonmouth to be repaired in a purpose-built workshop. The user pays a fixed price for a continuous guaranteed supply.

Hambrook's first customer for the scheme is a northern company carrying its products of bulk plastic packaging on thousands of pallets every week.

They hope to save more than 30% of the cost by using reconditioned pallets. The deal will be worth more than £300,000 to Hambrook.

'This is recycling at its best,' said Joint Managing Director, Martin Bond. 'It is possible only because we have expanded, with three new depots in the west of England – and three more planned in the new year.

'Every pallet that arrives is individually sorted and graded to meet the varying demands of customers.

'Companies seeking the BS5750 quality approval need a pallet source they can rely on, not a street corner supplier. Unsafe pallets can cause serious damage to goods, and make a whole load unsafe.'

Hambrook plans to extend its already national collection service to Holland soon.

Source: *Western Commerce*, No. 21, Dec '90 – Jan '91

a What is new about Hambrook's service?
b What problems can arise from buying new pallets?
c What kind of saving does Hambrook's first customer hope to make?
d How much is the deal worth?
e What can be the result of using unsafe pallets?

E Progress check

Complete the sentences with the most suitable alternative. Sometimes more than
one answer is correct.

1 We need...

  a ...to paint the lorries.
  b ...have the lorries painted.
  c ...to have the lorries painted.

2 I would like to apologise for _____ late.

  a arrive
  b to arrive
  c arriving

3 He _____ said that – it isn't true.

  a can't have
  b must have
  c wouldn't have

4 We _____ our security work to DIP Security.

  a under contract
  b sub-contract
  c contract out

5 You _____ let us know sooner.

  a would have
  b might have
  c should have

6 We service a number of international companies,
  _____ IBM, PSK and ICI.

  a such as
  b for example
  c as

7 The _____ is $55 per week.

  a lease
  b hire
  c rental

8 We handle most of our printing _____ .

  a in-house
  b in the house
  c ourselves

9 _____ to the increase in demand, the service
  has been extended.

  a Because
  b On account
  c Due

10 Could you give us a _____ for the work?

  a quote
  b price
  c charge

11 They do all _____ maintenance.

  a their
  b their own
  c themselves

12 We apologise for any inconvenience this _____ .

  a caused
  b might cause
  c might have caused

13 We _____ to get the engine reconditioned – it's
   very worn.

  a should
  b ought
  c must

14 There is really no need _____ .

  a apologise
  b to apologise
  c for apologising

15 They are specialists _____ recycling.

  a in
  b at
  c with

16 We hope to cut costs by around 7% using _____
   parts.

  a recycling
  b recycled
  c reconditioned

17 – The delivery still hasn't arrived.
   – I _____ apologise. It wasn't despatched until
     Friday.

  a did
  b do
  c must

18 _____ to their advertising people, sales are
   going well.

  a apparently
  b she said
  c according

ENTERTAINING

A Introduction

1 CONTENTS

2 REVISION

1 Revise common greetings and introductions. You meet the people below – say hello, introduce your colleagues, make conversation (about the weather, families, etc.).

a a client
b a relative
c an ex-colleague

2 Revise food and drink vocabulary. Can you name fives types of fruit, meat, vegetables and drink?

3 Form adverbs from these adjectives. Use them in sentences.

comfortable	*comfortably*	good	_____
extreme	_____	hard	_____
fast	_____	bad	_____

4 Revise adverbs of frequency. Put these adverbs in order of frequency and then use them in sentences.

> often   never   occasionally   sometimes   rarely   always

5 Revise reported speech. Then put these statements into reported speech.

a 'I'll get the drinks.' → He says _____ .
b 'Go home, you aren't well.' → She told him _____ .
c 'We are fully booked.' → They said _____ .

6 Revise common sporting activities. In which sport(s) do you use the following terms?

a goal   c pitch   e course
b table   d racket   f race

Can you complete these enquiries/invitations?

Do you play _____?
Would you like to go (for) _____?
How about a game of _____?

B Business hospitality

1 LISTENING

Revise adverbs of frequency.

1 Listen to the recording. Where does the speaker take visitors?

	usually	sometimes	occasionally	very rarely
to lunch in a local restaurant to dinner in central London sightseeing to the theatre to a football match to a cricket match				

2 How does this compare with the way that you entertain visitors in your company? Compare notes with a partner.

e.g. – Do you ever take clients sightseeing?
  – Yes, sometimes. / No, not very often.

  – We usually take them to a club.
  – So do we. / We do sometimes too.

2 READING

Some cultural 'do's and 'don't's

1 Read the 'Do's and 'Don't's for doing business with Japanese people. If you are Japanese, or if you have experience of doing business with the Japanese, is there anything you do not agree with?

Do

- If you are selling, sound supportive of all your company's products – even products that compete with those you are representing. To the Japanese, your loyalty to the company's overall operations is paramount.
- Find out beforehand how long a meeting is scheduled to last. Often, the Japanese schedule an hour and it is tricky to exit earlier – and even if you do, you may not have gone beyond lengthy preliminaries.
- Carry your business cards at all times – and remember that, in exchanging cards, you should offer your card first if the person you are meeting outranks you.
- Let your host take you to the lift after the meeting – he will feel he has not been fully hospitable if you suggest it is unnecessary.

Don't

- Interrupt your host. The Japanese take a while to find the right words even in Japanese: if you interrupt a significant pause, you may miss an important point.
- Show up late. Foreigners have an excuse in Tokyo – but if you really want to demonstrate you understand their market, do what the Japanese do and show up five minutes early.
- Sound boastful about your company or your products. Let facts speak for themselves. Your products can, for instance, be effectively boosted by quoting what other people say about them.
- Write on, or play with, your host's business card. Even for something as practical as noting your host's fax number, for instance, it is more diplomatic to let him write it on his card himself.

Giving advice

2 Make a list of 'Do's and 'Don't's for foreigners who are planning to do business with you. Discuss the list with a partner.

Useful language	
Never... / Always...	It is/isn't a good idea to...
You must never/always...	It is best (not) to...
You should never/always...	Make sure you (don't)...

3 LANGUAGE POINTS

> Revise *mustn't, needn't* and *don't have to* (see page 115).

1 Write *mustn't*, *needn't* or *don't have to* in the following sentences.

a We _____ show up late.
b You _____ hurry, there's plenty of time.
c It's an informal occasion, so you _____ wear a suit.
d You _____ bring a gift, but it's a good idea.
e I _____ forget to invite Mario.
f You _____ come if you don't want to.
g I _____ eat anything with sugar in it – I'm diabetic.
h We _____ finish the work till next week.

> *Was/Were going/hoping/planning to* and *was/were thinking of*

2 Note the following examples.

Changed plans

I was <u>going/hoping/planning to</u> buy a new car, but I couldn't afford it.
I was <u>thinking of</u> visiting Australia, but it didn't work out.

Suggestions and invitations

– I was <u>going/hoping/planning to</u> invite you out to dinner.
– That would be nice.
– I was <u>thinking of</u> getting tickets to the theatre.
– I'd like that very much.

3 Practise giving invitations. Work in pairs.

e.g. – Are you free [on Friday night]?
  – Yes, I am. / No, I'm not. Why?
  – I was going/hoping/planning to...
      thinking of...
  – I'd like that... / Oh, what a pity. I would have enjoyed that.

4 ACTIVITY

> *Prefer* and *would rather* (see page 115)

In pairs, talk about going out to dinner. **Partner A** is looking after **Partner B**.

Planning

> I thought we might...
> I was thinking of...
> Or would you rather...?
> What would you prefer?
> When would suit you?

▶

> I would love to.
> I don't mind. / I'm easy.
> I was hoping to...
> I'm free every evening except...

Diet considerations

> Is there anything you can't eat?

▶

> I don't eat [pork].
> I can't have [anything with sugar in it].
> I'm not allowed [dairy products].
> I'm on a (special) diet.
> I'm Jewish / (a) Moslem, so...

Etiquette

> What should I wear?
> Should I take/bring a gift?
> What do you suggest I take/bring?
> Should I arrive on time or [30 minutes] late/early?

▶

> It's (not) a good idea to...
> You don't have to...
> You needn't... (but...)

▲ 'I thought we might go to one of the restaurants near the office.'

C Hotels and restaurants

1 LISTENING

Ordering a meal

Listen to the recording, and refer to the menu. What do the speakers order?

	Starter	**Main course**
Ralph		
Mary		
Hiroshi		

The Brasserie

Menu
Served all day

Fresh fruit platter
A selection of sliced seasonal fruits with a choice of minted yoghurt dressing, or tropical sorbet

Smoked ham and strawberries

Scottish smoked salmon

Baked field mushrooms
Topped with a gratinée of mussels and shrimps glazed with cheese

Prawn salad
Cold-water prawns on a bed of sliced cucumber

French onion soup

---

8 oz sirloin steak
Served with a choice of spicy herb butter or green peppercorn sauce

Beef teriyaki
Slivers of beef fillet with mushrooms

Chicken Peri Peri
Barbecued spicy chicken breast, marinated with fresh chilli

Mixed seafood grill
Served with a bearnaise sauce.
(Check with your waiter for today's selection.)

Pacific tiger prawns
Served in the shell with your choice of garlic or lemon butter sauce

Vegetarian dish of the day

The above dishes are served with a selection of fresh seasonal vegetables, new potatoes, french fries or pilaff rice.

Apple pie

Fresh fruit salad

A selection of ice cream

Chocolate mousse

---

1 course £10   2 courses £14   3 courses £18

Prices include VAT. Service is not included.

2 ACTIVITY

Hotel entertaining: making a toast, tipping, etc. (see page 116)

Look at the stages of an evening out in a hotel. In pairs or small groups, put them in order, and discuss what people do and say. Is there anything else you would add to the list?

a Ask for the bill.

b Attract the waiter's attention and order the food.

c Check how your guests are going to get home.

d Ask for your table.

e Collect your coats and bags.

f Make a toast.

g Meet in the foyer and suggest a drink in the bar.

h Leave a tip.
i Order a round of drinks.
j Ask your guests to sit down (suggesting a seating arrangement).
k Say goodnight and thank you.
l Suggest moving to the restaurant.
m When the food arrives, ask people to start.
n Leave your coats and briefcases with the porter.

3 LANGUAGE POINTS

> Revise reported speech (see page 116).

1 Notice how the following words sometimes change when they are put into reported speech.

yesterday → the day before	here → there
tomorrow → the following day	this → that/the

2 Change the questions and statements into reported speech.

e.g. Have you stayed at this hotel before?
      He asked me <u>if I had stayed at the hotel before.</u>

a They have excellent conference facilities.
   He said _____ .
b Ask for a room with a sea view.
   He told me _____ .
c I'll have the beef.
   She said _____ .
d Don't order the fish. It isn't very good here.
   He advised me _____ .
e We went out for lunch yesterday.
   They said _____ .
f We are all going out for dinner tomorrow night.
   Ralph said _____ .
g How much do you usually tip?
   He asked _____ .

> *Say/Tell* and *speak/talk* (see page 116)

3 Complete these examples with *say*, *tell*, *speak* or *talk*. In some cases, there is more than one possibility.

a I _____ Dan to send them a fax.
b I _____ , 'Don't wait until tomorrow.'
c Can you _____ to your boss about it?
d We need to _____ about it.
e I _____ a little Polish, but not much.
f Let's _____ about it in the morning.
g What did they _____ to you?
h Can I _____ to Mary, please?

4 READING

> Quoting from a document

▲ 'Could you put the drinks on my bill?'

Work in pairs. Read the extracts from an article and then tell your partner about what you have read. Do you agree with the article?

Partner A: Your extract is on the right.
Partner B: Your extract is on page 117.

Useful language
It says that if/when you...
It states that if/when you...
It also says...
Does it say who pays when/if...?
What does it say about...?
It doesn't mention...

As a general rule, the person who invites someone else to a business meal should pay. There are exceptions to this rule, however.

Example: An employee asks a manager for lunch to discuss a work-related issue. The manager in this situation would pick up the tab, unless the employee insists.

Example: A customer asks a salesperson to join him for dinner, and the topic of discussion is strictly business. The salesperson is justified in incurring the meal as a business expense.

From *The Little Black Book of Business Etiquette*, by Michael C. Thomsett

D Corporate entertaining

1 READING

Revise the Simple Present in timetables.

Read the extract from the brochure. Then answer the questions. Would you use the club to entertain your clients or customers?

The Skyhigh Club

The club is located within the main hospitality complex. It is centrally located, giving a superb and uninterrupted view of the flying display. It is also conveniently located close to all the other show attractions.

Experienced management

The club will be run as a private suite where parties of between two and 50 can be catered for, at tables seating 10 guests. Your guests will be greeted on arrival and escorted to the Skyhigh Club where they will be met by the Skyhigh Reception Team. An experienced manager will be in the club at all times to ensure that your day runs smoothly.

Special access

Your guests will arrive by special VIP routes with a separate entrance to the airfield. Full details with maps and passes will be sent in June.

▲ The eight-hour flying-display will include at least 100 aircraft.

Event Information	
Airfield opens	8.00 am
Exhibition and Fun Park open	9.00 am
Arena displays commence	9.30 am
Flying display commences	10.00 am
Flying display finale	6.00 pm
Arena displays finish	7.00 pm
Exhibition and Fun Park close	7.30 pm
Airfield closes	8.00 pm

a Why will it be easy for visitors to find the club?
b How long does the flying display last?
c Is there more than one hospitality complex?
d What does VIP mean?
e What in your opinion is the strongest selling point in the extract?

2 LISTENING

A hospitality package

Listen to a client booking hospitality at a golf tournament. What changes to the standard package does she require?

Birch Meadows
Hospitality

The deluxe hospitality package includes:
• a luxury air-conditioned suite for clients;
• floral arrangements;
• use of telephones and facsimile machines;
• a cordoned-off area with comfortable seating;
• an excellent view of the proceedings;
• toilet facilities;
• admission charges;
• private parking facilities;
• souvenir programmes.

Superb catering to include:
• morning coffee;
• a full four-course lunch;
• afternoon tea;
• full bar facilities;
• music to accompany meals, by arrangement.

£150 per person
(fully inclusive)

3 LANGUAGE POINTS

> Revise the spelling and position of adverbs (see page 118).

1 Change the adjectives to adverbs and put them in these sentences.

a I agree with you.
(total) _____

b The reception went well.
(extreme) _____

c I read the information.
(quick) _____

d We take visitors to the theatre.
(rare) _____

e I drove to work this morning.
(slow) _____

f Driving conditions were difficult.
(terrible) _____

g She organised everything.
(brilliant) _____

h She didn't forget anything.
(surprising) _____

> Comparative adverbs (see page 118)

2 Put these adverbs into the comparative form.

a When we have the right team, the event runs _____ (smoothly).

b If you want to get to work on time, you should get up _____ (early).

c We have to work _____ (hard) because we're a small team.

d Sales rose _____ (slowly) in the second quarter.

e He is no good in a team – he works _____ (well) on his own.

f I play about once a month – I used to play _____ (often).

g You drive _____ (badly) than I do.

h I really need your reply _____ (soon) than that.

> Some sports vocabulary

3 Which sports can the phrases below relate to? (Each phrase can relate to more than one sport.)

> snooker boxing wrestling swimming golf badminton
> table tennis squash football sailing rugby motor racing

a They're playing well.
b Good shot.
c It wasn't a very good fight.
d Well played!
e Did you enjoy the match?
f It was a very close race.
g What a terrible pass!
h Which round is it?
i The first half was better.

4 ACTIVITY

> Booking hospitality
>
> Revise making suggestions (see page 118).

In pairs, practise booking a hospitality package. Decide on an event.

e.g. a tennis tournament
a race meeting
a football match
an open air concert

Partner A: You work for a hospitality company. Adapt the information in 2 LISTENING to suit the event.

Partner B: You are interested in taking some clients to the event. Your information is on page 118.

E Progress check

Complete the sentences with the most suitable alternative. Sometimes more than one answer is correct.

1 Do you play _____ ?

  a swimming
  b golf
  c chess

2 Can I _____ a table for four people?

  a order
  b book
  c make

3 I was _____ to get tickets for the match.

  a going
  b thinking
  c hoping

4 How much do you usually _____ the waiter?

  a pay
  b give
  c tip

5 Have you thought of _____ your hospitality through us?

  a buying
  b booking
  c renting

6 We _____ clients to the circus.

  a often don't take
  b don't often take
  c don't take often

7 The _____ includes tickets to all the main events.

  a deal
  b packet
  c package

8 Does it _____ what the price is?

  a say
  b tell
  c mention

9 Our team _____ that everything is organised efficiently.

  a work
  b make sure
  c ensure

10 _____ us something about the company.

  a Say
  b Speak
  c Tell

11 You _____ wear a suit, but it's a good idea.

  a needn't
  b don't have to
  c mustn't

12 I am working very _____ these days.

  a hard
  b hardly
  c harder

13 I'd _____ go sightseeing.

  a like
  b prefer
  c rather

14 Tom said he _____ his umbrella.

  a has lost
  b had lost
  c is losing

15 If you want it _____ than that, you will have to pay extra.

  a quicker
  b quicklier
  c more quickly

16 What _____ I bring as a gift?

  a should
  b must
  c ought

17 He says the booking was confirmed _____ .

  a yesterday
  b tomorrow
  c the following day

18 It's best _____ late.

  a don't arrive
  b to not arrive
  c not to arrive

A Introduction

1 CONTENTS

A Introduction
B Setting up a meeting
C Procedure
D Follow-up
E Progress check

MEETINGS

2 REVISION

1 Revise the use of *so*, *neither*, *too* and *either*. Then agree with the following, using each word once.

a I think the meeting is at 10.00. ——————————————————————
b I don't think John is coming. ——————————————————————
c I believe he is away. ——————————————————————
d I don't believe it is possible. ——————————————————————

2 Revise conditional sentences. Complete the following examples.

a What will you do if _____?
b If the weather is good _____.
c If they don't come _____.
d I won't buy it if _____.

3 Revise prepositions. Complete the following sentences.

a Can you make the meeting _____ the 23rd?
b It'll be _____ lunch some time.
c It's a meeting _____ the VZ contract.
d Was John _____ the meeting?

4 Change the following question into reported speech.

'Mary, could you take the minutes, please?'

a She asked _____
b She told _____
c She wanted _____
d She said _____

5 Number these responses from 1 to 4, where 1 = *I strongly agree*, and 4 = *I strongly disagree*. Then use them in short exchanges.

a Are you sure?
b I don't think you're right.
c That's right.
d I don't agree.

e.g. – I think _____.
    – I'm afraid I don't agree.

6 Revise the vocabulary of punctuation. Then point out examples of the following in a text.

a a full stop   d a sentence
b a question mark   e a comma
c a capital letter   f an exclamation mark

B Setting up a meeting

1 READING

Arranging the time and place

John Shipman is organising a meeting. He wants Phillip Lux to be present. Read the exchange of faxes and write in when they were sent.

i 21st May, 10 am
ii 21st May, 3.30 pm
iii 22nd May, 11 am

Then write in the sender's and receiver's names.

a
```
Time / Date _____

Dear _____ ,

Sorry to hear about Friday. But don't worry,
Saturday lunch would be fine. I've been in touch
with Kaz and Tony and they would love to see you
then. Could you come to my office at 11 o'clock on
Saturday morning? We need to talk about the sales
report. We could have a couple of hours to go over
some papers, and then have lunch in the Crown at
about 1.00. How does that sound? If I don't hear
from you, I'll assume that everything is OK.

Hope to see you on Saturday.

_____
```

b
```
Time / Date _____

To: _____
Are you still OK for Friday? Tony and Kaz are
coming, although they are going to be a little bit
late - they said they'd try and be here by 3.15 at
the latest. Could you let me know by the weekend?
I'll be on 0101-921-637.

Yours,

_____
```

c
```
Time / Date _____

Thank you for the fax. I'm sorry, but it looks as
if Friday is going to be difficult. I've got some
people coming over from Mexico and I promised to
show them round the site that day - I'm afraid I
can't get out of it.
How long are Tony and Kaz going to be with you for?
If they are planning to stay for the weekend, I
suggest that we all meet up for lunch on Saturday.
Anyway - let me know.

Best wishes,

_____
```

2 LISTENING

Last-minute changes
Revise *had better* (see page 120).

Phillip calls John Shipman with a last-minute change of plan. Listen to the recording and number the final details in the right order.

a John gives Phillip a lift to a hotel near Heathrow.   [   ]
b Kaz and Tony fly from Heathrow.   [   ]
c Phillip flies to Belgium with the Mexican clients.   [1]
d The Mexican clients fly to Madrid direct from Brussels.   [   ]
e Kaz, Tony, John and Phillip have lunch together.   [   ]
f Philip flies to London.   [   ]

3 LANGUAGE POINTS

To be able to (see page 120)

1 Complete the sentences with *can* or *could* where possible. Where *can* and *could* aren't appropriate, use *be able to*.

e.g. Would you <u>be able to</u> meet me on the 24th?

a I _____ (*not*) take the minutes – I'll be away.
b Is she going to _____ make the meeting?

c I'd like to _____ type properly.
d We should _____ meet on 27th.
e It looks as if we _____ use room 207.
f I enjoy _____ walk to the office.
g I _____ (*not*) post it – it wasn't ready.
h You must _____ reach him somehow.

Look as if/though and *sound as if/though*

▲ 'It looks as though Monday is going to be difficult.'

2 Change the sentences, using *look as if/though* and *sound as if/though*.

e.g. I think everyone can come.
    It <u>looks as if everyone can come.</u>

a I have the impression that you don't agree.
   You _____ .
b I think we'd better postpone the meeting.
   It _____ .
c It seems that the room isn't available.
   It _____ .
d I think you need a holiday.
   You _____ .
e Your car seems to need repairing.
   Your car _____ .
f His accent sounds Spanish.
   He _____ .

4 ACTIVITY

Agendas

1 Which of these agendas is more familiar to you? Compare them with the agendas you use.

1) Department reports
2) Co-operation with RSK
3) Update on ISO project
4) Report on new computer system
5) AOB

AGENDA
Management Meeting
Room 406, Queen's House
at 10.00, on 24 July

1 Apologies for absence
2 Minutes of the last meeting
3 Matters arising from the minutes
4 Monthly sales report (enclosed)
5 Research and development budget (enclosed)
   a Report by Finance Committee (enclosed)
   b Review
6 Any other business
7 Date of next meeting

Three enclosures: Monthly sales report
            Research and development budget for next year
            Report on projected R&D spending

Punctuation (see page 120)

Rearranging a meeting (see page 120)

2 In small groups, draw up an agenda. Agree on the items. Then dictate the agenda.

3 Now set up a meeting.

a Fix a time and place.
b Notify everyone.
c Circulate the agenda.
d Rearrange the time and/or place. (Someone has a change of plan.)
e Call to check that everyone can make it.

Useful language

Are you (still) OK for...?
It's taking place at [2 pm] on...
We're meeting to discuss...
I'll send you a copy of the agenda.
I'm having some problems at this end.
The meeting has been put off till...
It looks as if [Friday] is going to be difficult.
Would you be able to meet at/on...?
We'd better meet on/at... instead.

C Procedure

1 LISTENING

Phrases used in meetings (see page 137)

1 Listen to the four extracts from meetings and answer the questions.

a Had the people at the meeting met before?
Why was the speaker late for the meeting?

b Who is going to take the minutes?
What is the purpose of the meeting?

c What are they talking about?
Does Mark think the contractors are trustworthy?

d Is the proposal approved by the meeting?
How does Sarah vote?

▲ 'Mark, what's your opinion on all this?'

2 Refer to the list of phrases commonly used in meetings, on page 137. Which of the phrases are used in the dialogues?

2 LANGUAGE POINTS

The Second Conditional: *Would it be better if we started earlier?* (see page 121)

If I were you... (see page 121)

1 Rewrite the following sentences using the Second Conditional.

e.g. We don't have enough spare parts. We'll have to stop the machines.
If we had enough spare parts, we wouldn't have to stop the machines.

a We don't pay them enough. They are going to go on strike.
_____

b We should pay off our bank loans. Then we won't have the bank on our backs.
_____

c I would ban smoking at work, but I'm not in charge.
_____

d We don't have ISO accreditation. Our customers will stop buying from us.
_____

e We don't get any work done. We have too many meetings.
_____

f We spend too much on entertaining clients. There is no money for training.
_____

g They smoke – that's why they don't support the ban.
_____

h You should give up smoking. I would, in your position.
_____

Expressing agreement and disagreement

2 Do these phrases indicate agreement or disagreement? Which ones can be used neutrally? Which ones are informal?

	Agreement	Disagreement
Absolutely.	✔	
Come off it!		
Rubbish!		
I'm not sure I agree with that.		
Definitely.		
I don't know.		
I don't agree with that.		
That's right.		
I'm afraid I disagree completely.		
I agree with you up to a point.		
I agree with most of what you say.		
Yes, but...		
Not necessarily.		

3 In pairs, practise agreeing, disagreeing and giving neutral responses.

| I (don't) think/believe... In my opinion/view... I'm in favour of... I'm opposed to... | ◄► | Absolutely. I'm not sure I agree completely. I'm sorry, but that simply isn't right. |

3 READING AND LISTENING

Smoking in the workplace

1 Read the article about smoking in the workplace. Do you agree with the French policy? Make notes in preparation for a meeting to discuss the implications for your business.

FRENCH BAN IS CASE OF LAISSEZ-FUMER

Millions of French smokers are wondering what awaits them when they return to work on Monday after a new law comes into effect at midnight tomorrow establishing non-smoking as the rule in all enclosed public places.

The law will have its most serious impact in offices and factories, where people will no longer be able to smoke in common work areas.

Smoking will also be banned in communal areas such as canteens and reception rooms, and employers will have to set aside special sections to accommodate their smokers.

'The main principle of the law is to protect non-smokers,' says Guillaume Pepy, Chief of Staff for the Minister of Labour, Martine Aubry. 'We cannot ignore any longer the evidence of cancer caused by smoking and also passive smoking.'

Official figures put smoking-related deaths in France last year at 54,000.

Source: *The Guardian*, 31/10/92

2 Listen to the recording. The speakers have read the article. Tick [✓] the items they want on the agenda.

Items for the agenda:
- **Production considerations**
- **Special areas for smokers**
- **Company policy on smoking ✓**
- **Counselling for smokers**
- **Resistance of smokers**
- **Penalties**
- **Reaction of hourly-paid workers**
- **Positive action (anti-smoking posters, etc.)**

4 ACTIVITY

Referring to documents: *If you look at line 4...* (see page 121)

3 Hold a meeting to discuss smoking in the workplace.

a Adapt the above agenda to your needs.
b Use the list of phrases on page 137 to help you.
c Refer to the article above, as necessary.

e.g. In the third paragraph, line five, it says...
       The third sentence says...   etc.

D Follow-up

1 READING

Follow-up to a meeting

1 Read the letter. Is Fabio Mercotzi senior, junior or equal in position to Pilar Hernandez?

> Fabio,
>
> It was good to see you last week. I think that the meeting went very well, and that we managed to cover a lot of ground. I have already contacted the contractor as agreed, and I put your suggestions about delivery procedures to him.
>
> He thought they were a good idea in principle. He suggested that we give them specific details of what we want, and they will draw up a plan for us to consider. I said you were sending them a more detailed outline of your proposals.
>
> Not so much luck on the money question though. They want to charge us for anything which was not in the original contract. But I haven't given up. I'm meeting their MD next week to discuss our credit limit, so I'll raise the matter then.
>
> Hope you received the action steps. Looking forward to receiving the notes you promised on how to handle next week's meeting.
>
> With best wishes,
>
> *Pilar Hernandez*

Summarising action to be taken:
AB to call CD, etc.

2 Tick the action steps referred to in the letter above.

> **SITE MANAGEMENT MEETING**
> 17 April
>
> cc Fabio Mercotzi, Harry Gross, Pilar Hernandez
>
> **Action**
> * PH to contact NAK Supplies:
>   - re. changes in delivery procedures;
>   - to enquire about price reductions.
> * PH to arrange meeting with NAK's MD to discuss credit limits.
> * FM to send a more detailed outline of proposal to NAK and HG.
> * HG to check how the changes affect the insurance position.
> * FM to send PH notes on handling the money
> * question.

2 LISTENING

A follow-up phone call

Listen to the follow-up phone conversation between Pilar Hernandez and Fabio Mercotzi. Then answer the questions.

a Has Fabio received Pilar's letter?
b What was Pilar expecting to receive from Fabio?
c Why hasn't Fabio sent anything?
d Will NAK be happy to make the changes for a small fee?
e Why does Harry Gross need a copy of the proposals?
f What does Pilar promise to do at the end of the call?

3 LANGUAGE POINTS

More reported speech (see page 122)

1 Change the following sentences to indirect speech.

e.g. 'It would be a good idea if she circulated the agenda in advance.'
Max wanted <u>her to circulate the agenda in advance.</u>
He suggested <u>that she should circulate the agenda in advance.</u>

a 'I think Owen should chair the meeting.'
Anita said _____ .
She proposed _____ .
b 'Who is going to take the minutes?'
Ivan asked _____ .
He wanted _____ .
c 'Why don't we demand compensation?'
Lupe wondered _____ .
She suggested _____ .
d 'I think we should cancel the order.'
Franz thought _____ .
He proposed _____ .

Verbs followed by the infinitive

2 In pairs, talk about commitments and decisions, using the verbs in the box.

I	agreed	to...
	arranged	
We	decided	not to...
	managed	
My assistant	offered	
	promised	
etc.	remembered	
	forgot	
	hoped	
	planned	

e.g. We didn't manage to cover all the points, so we agreed to meet again tomorrow.

3 In pairs, discuss a meeting.

Partner A: Answer questions about a meeting you have attended recently.
Partner B: Find out about the meeting. See the questions on page 122.

4 ACTIVITY

Checking action steps

▲ 'That's all taken care of.'

Practise following up a meeting. In pairs or groups, decide on a number of actions to be taken following a meeting.

a List the action steps.
b Allocate the steps.
c Have a follow-up meeting to check on progress.

Useful language
Did you manage to...?
Were you able to...?
What's the position with/on...?
How are you getting on with...?
It's all taken care of.
I'm hoping/planning to do it on...
Which (letter)?
To be honest, I've been so busy...

E Progress check

Complete the sentences with the most suitable alternative. Sometimes more than one answer is correct.

1 The Finance Director _____ that I should chair the meeting.

   a suggested
   b said
   c wanted

2 I'd go to the meeting if I _____ you.

   a were
   b would be
   c am

3 To be _____ , I can't find their letter.

   a honestly
   b frank
   c true

4 We are meeting to _____ about the sales figures.

   a discuss
   b talk
   c speak

5 Who is going to take _____ ? Could you do it, Ursula?

   a the minutes
   b the agenda
   c the vote

6 It looks as if we _____ use room 407.

   a can
   b could
   c will be able

7 Did you remember _____ the minutes?

   a circulate
   b circulating
   c to circulate

8 Our main _____ is to agree the contract.

   a aim
   b topic
   c purpose

9 I can't make the meeting on Friday. Can we _____ till next week?

   a put it off
   b cancel it
   c postpone it

10 We didn't _____ to cover all the points.

    a able
    b manage
    c succeed

11 We had better _____ at the airport.

    a to meet
    b meeting
    c meet

12 I have to say that I am opposed _____ the proposal.

    a of
    b for
    c to

13 If they _____ , there wouldn't be a problem.

    a wouldn't smoke
    b didn't smoke
    c smoked

14 I enclose a copy of the action points, _____ .

    a as I promised
    b as you promised
    c as promised

15 (On a dictaphone.) 'I enclose a copy of the agenda _____ .'

    a full stop
    b question mark
    c comma

16 – What it says in the third paragraph is nonsense!
    – I agree _____ a point.

    a with
    b to
    c up to

17 We are _____ the meeting in room 400.

    a having
    b taking place
    c holding

18 How are you getting _____ the minutes?

    a on
    b with
    c on with

TRAVEL

A Introduction

1 CONTENTS

A Introduction
B Arranging a visit
C Abroad on business
D Reporting back
E Progress check

2 REVISION

1 Revise giving directions.
Then direct a visitor to:

a your place of work;
b your office.

e.g. Leave the motorway at
Junction 4.
Go through these swing
doors – it's the first
door on the left.

2 Name ten countries and their capital cities.

3 Revise common hotel vocabulary. Then use the phrases in the box in sentences.

e.g. I'd like a single room on the first floor.

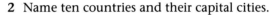

a single room   a cup of coffee   room service
ground floor   very noisy   vacancy   two nights

4 Revise means of transport. Complete the pairs. Then use the phrases in sentences.

e.g. When I'm travelling on business, I normally go by plane.

a by train   _____
b _____   by road
c by plane   _____
d by ferry   _____

5 Revise how to talk about future plans and events. Answer these questions. Then ask three similar questions about the future, using *going to*, the Present Continuous, and the Present Simple.

a What are you going to do tomorrow?
b Are you doing anything special this evening?
c What time do you finish work today?

6 Note these examples of *will*. Decide whether *will* is used for a promise, a prediction, or a sudden decision. Then give more examples of each.

a In that case, I'll wait.
b I expect we will get the contract.
c Don't worry. I'll send the information tomorrow.

B Arranging a visit

1 READING

| A letter of introduction |

1 Read the letter. What is the reason for Ms Braun's visit to the States?

---

rfm GmbH

OTTOSTRASSE 47, D4000 DÜSSELDORF

Dr J.C.Keller
President
Blue Ribbon Inc.
14940 Magnolia Blvd.
Boston
MA 91503 USA

Dear Dr Keller,

I am writing (**a**) _____ behalf of the managing Director of RFM, Ms Rita Braun, to inform you that she will be visiting Boston (**b**) _____ 11 and 12 July and that she would very much like to arrange an appointment (**c**) _____ a member of your staff.

As our organisation also specialises (**d**) _____ training for health and safety, Ms Braun is keen (**e**) _____ discuss possible future co-operation (**f**) _____ you. We are very interested (**g**) _____ establishing a relationship with an American partner.

If you would like (**h**) _____ meet Ms Braun, please let me know when would be most convenient (**i**) _____ you.

Ms Braun will be staying (**j**) _____ the Farrington Inn while she is in Boston.

Yours sincerely,

Linda B Gaddum

Linda Gaddum
Personal Assistant

---

2 Fill in the gaps in the text with the words below.

| on   on   in   in   with   with   for   at   to   to |

2 LISTENING

| Directions from an airport |

Listen to the recording and number the directions by taxi in the right order.

---

rfm GmbH

OTTOSTRASSE 47, D4000 DÜSSELDORF

Dear Sir,

Please send me directions on how to get to the Farrington Inn. I will be arriving at Logan airport.

Yours faithfully,

R Braun

Ms Rita Braun

ATTN. Rita Braun

THE FARRINGTON
The Sensible Alternative to Hotel Prices

DIRECTIONS FROM LOGAN AIRPORT

Thank you for deciding to stay with us while you are in Boston. PLEASE call us as soon as you arrive here, especially if your plane is early or late. We look forward to meeting you.

BY TAXI

• Go down Harvard, and take your first left again, onto FARRINGTON AVE.
• Leave Mass Pike here. (The toll is 50 cents.) The exit ramp merges onto a street. Follow the signs to ALLSTON.
• Tell the cab driver to take the SUMNER TUNNEL, and then get on the EXPRESSWAY SOUTH, which takes you to the MASSACHUSETTS TURNPIKE (Mass Pike).
• We are the fifth house on the right. We have two bright red doors. Go in the door on the right, number 23.
• Take the Mass Pike west to the first exit, signposted to ALLSTON-CAMBRIDGE.
• Go to the fourth set of lights, and turn left. This is HARVARD AVE – there is an antique store on the corner.

3 LANGUAGE POINTS

The Future Continuous: *I'll be working in Boston…* (see page 123)

1 Compare these examples.

I'm leaving on Friday.
I'm going to leave on Friday.
I'll leave on Friday if I can get on a flight.
I'll be leaving on Friday.

2 Work in pairs. Find out what your partner expects to be doing:

- this time tomorrow;
- this time next week;
- this time next month;
- this time next year;
- in two years' time.

e.g. This time next week, I'll be celebrating my promotion.
I expect I'll still be working in the bank this time next year.

3 Complete the sentences with an appropriate future form of the verb.

e.g. <u>They're going to</u> win the contract.

a _____ to Budapest next week?
b _____ if I can arrange it.
c What _____ this afternoon?
d I _____ some clients.
e When _____ (leave)?
f I think they _____ at about 5.30.
g I _____ this afternoon.
h The last post _____ at 4.15 today.

While, during and *for*

4 Compare these examples.

I will be in Boston <u>for</u> two days.
I hope we will meet <u>during</u> my stay.
My assistant will be here <u>while</u> I am away.

5 Complete these examples.

a Did you do much sightseeing _____ you were there?
b We don't want any calls _____ the meeting.
c Will you be seeing John _____ you are in Paris?
d There were no trains _____ three hours.
e She usually visits the States a couple of times _____ the summer.
f Next month, I'll be working in Hungary _____ two weeks.
g I don't like being contacted about work _____ I'm on holiday.
h Will you have time to visit us _____ your stay?

4 ACTIVITY

Checking the details of an itinerary

Work in pairs.
Partner A: You receive a call from **Partner B** who needs details of your forthcoming visit to Malaysia. Your information is below.
Partner B: Your information is on page 124.

ITINERARY

23rd Nov	Arrival at Kuala Lumpur airport. Flight LF 234 at 2.30 pm.
24th Nov	Visit to Zin Go Wan.
25th Nov	Transfer by car to Ipoh.
26th Nov	Meeting with Mr Brown.
27th Nov	Return to Kuala Lumpur airport. Singapore Airlines, flight SQ 739 at 11.30 am to Singapore.

C Abroad on business

1 READING

Advice on jet lag

1 Read the text. Is the advice in line with your experience?

Flying between London and New York

Westbound:

* Take the last flight of the day from London. This allows a reasonable day's work prior to departure.
* Stay awake during the flight, or just have a short nap.
* Avoid alcohol, tea and coffee, all of which interfere with sleep.
* Go to bed within three hours of arrival.
* Fatigue from the flight is usually enough to ensure that you sleep. You might wake early – often at around 4 am or 5 am local time. To counteract this, take a mild sleeping pill.
* If you do get up early, avoid arranging important meetings at the end of the day.

Eastbound:

* Flights usually depart early in the evening between 6 and 9 pm. Local time on arrival is early morning.
* Eat a light meal before taking off.
* Ask the cabin crew not to disturb you.
* Get a good night's sleep during the flight: consider taking a mild sleeping pill as soon as you board the aircraft.
* If you are travelling from the east coast of the United States, take the smallest effective dose. Standard doses are based on a likely 8-hour night and you may arrive feeling drugged rather than refreshed.
* Once back in Britain, you might wake late in the morning and find it difficult to get to sleep at the normal time.

Source: *How to Stay Healthy Abroad*, by Richard Dawood

2 Adapt the advice for someone travelling from:

a your country to New York;
b New York to Moscow.

3 In pairs, discuss how you cope with the following:

a jet lag;   c sleeping on planes;
b working in transit;   d eating meals at irregular hours.

Revise *easy/difficult to*, etc. (see page 125).

e.g. – It's easy to cope with jet lag.
       – Do you think so? I find it quite difficult.
OR: – I find it difficult to sleep on planes.
       – Do you? I don't. I just take a sleeping pill.

2 LANGUAGE POINTS

When, as soon as, while, before, etc. in future sentences (see page 125)

1 Note the following examples.

I'll take a pill as soon as I'm on the plane.
When I reach New York, I'll go to bed.
Will you be seeing John before he leaves?
I won't have much time while I'm at the conference.

2 Write the sentences.

a I see her / give her your regards
   (when) _____

b I not sleep / get to New York
   (until) _____

c be able to do it / you go?
   (before) _____

d I get to my hotel / have a bath
   (as soon as) _____

e you be working / you in France?
   (while) _____

f let you know / they call the flight
   (when) _____

g I call you / taxi here
   (as soon as) _____

h Where you be staying / in Berlin?
   (while) _____

Some travel vocabulary

3 Put the words into an appropriate group. Some words can go in more than one group.

> jet lag   customs   travel sickness   overbooking   transfer desk
> long-haul flight   hydrofoil   ferry terminal   dual carriageway
> toll bridge   duty free   filling station   runway   landing
> parking meter   buffet car   chauffeur   level crossing

air   _jet lag, customs_ _____
      _____

sea   _customs_ _____
      _____

land _customs_ _____
      _____

3 LISTENING AND ACTIVITY

Some common travel situations

▲ 'Is the flight delayed?'

1 Listen to the dialogues and answer the questions.

A hotel check-in
a Does the hotel have a single room with a bath?
b What does the £120 include?
c Where does Mr Vanta want the bill to be sent?

A railway booking office
d When is the passenger travelling?
e Why is it a good idea to reserve a seat?
f How does he want to pay?

A filling station
g What does the customer need to pay for?
h Why does the attendant recommend the B road?
i Where does he have to leave the main road?

A car hire firm
j What kind of car is the customer looking for?
k What do the company's rates include?
l When does he want the car?

2 In pairs, identify the situations where these phrases might be heard. Some may be used in several situations. Practise the situations you meet most often.

a I have a reservation in the name of Tuck.
b A day return to London, please.
c Can I check my bags through to Edinburgh?
d They sell them in the gift shop.
e Turn right, then left, then right again.
f Have you got any Italian lire?
g They're very nice. How much are they?
h I have to leave tomorrow morning before breakfast.
i Can you take the next turning on the left?
j It's a present for my daughter.
k Does that include insurance?
l Is there a toilet I can use?

D Reporting back

1 READING

Some acronyms (see page 126)

Rankings: *second largest*, etc. (see page 126)

Work in pairs.

Partner A: Read the notes on Brazil and the covering letter. Then call **Partner B** for further details. Ask about:

- background information on Mercosul;
- more population figures;
- further information on the size of the regions;
- more information on the regions' main industries;
- additional information on export possibilities;
- a specific figure for GDP;
- further details on Rio Grande do Sul.

Partner B: You wrote the report. Further details are on page 126.

Dear Mario,

I enclose some notes on my recent trip to Brazil. Our agent in São Paulo was very helpful. I made some good contacts. Please get back to me if you need further details.

Yours,

Alex

Brazil is the largest country in Latin America. It is a founder member of the Latin American Free Trade Association (LAFTA), and a key member of Mercosul. The country is divided into nine major economic areas, the wealthiest of which are:

São Paulo
São Paulo is the same size as the United Kingdom and has the heaviest concentration of industrial firms in Latin America. It accounts for 55% of Brazil's industrial output and 43% of its GDP. It offers major opportunities for direct export and joint venture operations, particularly in the more advanced areas of technology.

Rio de Janeiro
Known as the 'gateway to Brazil', this is the second largest industrial centre in the region. It has a population of approximately 14 million, its main industries being offshore oil and gas, chemicals, petrochemicals, steel, cement and alcohol.

Minas Gerais
In terms of economic activity, this is the third most important state in Brazil. The main industries in Minas Gerais are mining, steel production and capital goods, and it offers major opportunities for export and technology transfer, particularly in the mining, metallurgy, food processing, biotechnology, chemicals, and micro-electronics industries.

Other major trading areas are Espirito Santo which has seen growth rates far higher than the national average, and Parana, the base for more than 170 manufacturing firms, and Rio Grande do Sul.

2 LISTENING

Talking about a trip

Points of the compass

1 Notice these examples:

It is north-east of Chelyabinsk.
It is to the south-west of Nevtchugansk.
It is in the north-east of Siberia

2 Listen to an oil engineer talking about a recent visit to Nevtchugansk in Siberia. Does he like the place? Are these statements true [T] or false [F]?

a He went by train from Moscow.   [   ]
b It was a comfortable trip.   [   ]
c He spent about three days there.   [   ]
d Nevtchugansk has a population of approximately 100,000.   [   ]
e Chelyabinsk is south-east of Nevtchugansk.   [   ]
f He took his cold weather clothes.   [   ]

3 LANGUAGE POINTS

A long way, not far, a long time and not long

In case (see page 126)

1 In pairs, practise asking about distances and times.

e.g. – How far is it to [Lima] from here?
   – It's a long way. It's about 1400 kilometres.
   – How long does it take to get there?
   – It depends how you travel...

2 Write *if* or *in case* in the gaps.

e.g. I'll wear my cold weather gear <u>if</u> it snows.
   I'll take my cold weather gear, <u>in case</u> it snows.

a I'll get to the airport by 12, _____ the plane is early.
b _____ the plane is early, they will have to wait for us.
c I'll write my report today, _____ they need it tomorrow.
d _____ I finish it before you go home, I'll let you have a copy.
e _____ the airline lose my bags, I'll claim on the insurance.
f I'd better insure my bags, _____ I lose them.
g I'll book a table for four, _____ John comes.
h We'll need a table for four _____ John comes.

4 ACTIVITY

Staying in hotels

1 What is important to you when you stay in a hotel? Complete the questionnaire. Compare notes with other members of your group.
2 Recommend a hotel you have stayed at to the rest of the group.

▲ A fully equipped office in a business suite at the Copthorne Tara Hotel, Kensington, West London

	MOST IMPORTANT → LEAST IMPORTANT
Friendly service at reception	5 4 3 2 1
Prompt service at reception	5 4 3 2 1
Clear information about hotel services	5 4 3 2 1
Cleanliness of the room	5 4 3 2 1
Cosiness of the room	5 4 3 2 1
Standard of equipment in the room and bathroom	5 4 3 2 1
Quality of food	5 4 3 2 1
Friendly service in the restaurant	5 4 3 2 1
Prompt service in the restaurant	5 4 3 2 1
Atmosphere in the night club	5 4 3 2 1
Value for money	5 4 3 2 1

Reporting back on a trip

3 In pairs or groups, report back on a trip you have made. Comment on:

• the area;
• the trip;
• the accommodation.

Useful language

Where exactly is it?
What is it like?
Is it far from...?
What's the population?
What are the main industries?
How did you get there?
What were you doing there?
How long were you there?
Where did you stay?

E Progress check

Complete the sentences. In certain cases, there is more than one possible answer.

1 São Paulo accounts for 55 _____ of Brazil's industrial output.

   a per cents
   b per cent
   c pro cent

2 There are some _____ on the Glasgow road.

   a backlogs
   b congestion
   c roadworks

3 Where will you be staying _____ your stay?

   a while
   b during
   c for

4 I _____ some good contacts in Rio.

   a made
   b took
   c did

5 Does the price of the room _____ breakfast?

   a take
   b consist
   c include

6 It is _____ state in the region.

   a the third important
   b the third more important
   c the third most important

7 What _____ this time next year?

   a will you do
   b are you doing
   c will you be doing

8 Do you find _____ to sleep on planes?

   a difficulty
   b difficult
   c it difficult

9 It is _____ from Rio.

   a far
   b long
   c a long way

10 I'll go to bed as soon as I _____ to New York.

   a get
   b will get
   c will be getting

11 Are you familiar _____ Boston?

   a with
   b for
   c to

12 London is _____ of the UK.

   a south-east
   b in the south-east
   c to the south-east

13 What time do you _____ to Madrid?

   a arrive
   b get
   c reach

14 The hotel is three star _____ five star.

   a rather
   b rather than
   c more than

15 I'll insure my luggage _____ I lose it.

   a if
   b in case
   c because

16 I am writing _____ .

   a on Mr Smith's behalf
   b on behalf of Mr Smith
   c on the behalf of Mr Smith

17 Where will you be staying _____ you are in Paris?

   a while
   b when
   c till

18 _____ the signs to Chelsea.

   a Take
   b Turn
   c Follow

MONEY AND FINANCE

A Introduction

1 CONTENTS

A Introduction
B Personal finances
C Company finances
D Payment
E Progress check

2 REVISION

1 Revise common financial vocabulary. Then complete the sentences with the verbs in the box.

a Our sales reps _____ £24,000 per year.
b We _____ £135,000 a month on heating bills.
c The new equipment _____ £2.7 million.
d Our accountant _____ $500 an hour.
e We _____ $1100 a week in rent.

cost earn
pay spend
charge

2 Express these percentages as fractions. Write them in examples.

a 75% _____   c 50% _____
b 25% _____   d 33% _____

3 Revise the Passive form. Rewrite the sentences in the passive. What questions could these be answers to?

a They founded the company in 1962. _____
b They pay us by cheque. _____
c We print our brochures in Korea. _____
d I'll finish the work by three o'clock. _____

4 Revise the use of *much, many, a lot (of), little* and *few*. Then talk about expenditure.

I/We spend a lot on _____ .
I/We buy very few _____ .
I/We don't spend much on _____ .
I/We don't buy very much _____ .

5 Revise common banking terms. How many compound nouns can you make with these words? Use them in sentences.

e.g. Our bank account is £10,000 in credit.

account balance bank book card cash
cheque credit dispenser exchange interest
number rate statement travellers

6 Name the currencies you know. Discuss exchange rates.

e.g. How many pesetas are there to the Deutschmark?

B Personal finances

1 LISTENING

Personal expenditure

Do and *did* for emphasis (see page 127)

1 Listen to the recording. Tick [✔] the items which the speaker spends money on.

2 What do you spend money on?

charities	[ ]	theatre and other arts events	[ ]
eating out	[ ]	stocks and shares	[ ]
clothes	[ ]	children	[ ]
foreign travel	[ ]	cars	[ ]
religious activities	[ ]	books	[ ]
DIY	[ ]	antiques	[ ]
food and groceries	[ ]	sport: sailing, golf, etc.	[ ]

2 LANGUAGE POINTS

Some common financial vocabulary

1 Complete the sentences using these verbs.

afford	cash	clear	earn
go	keep	pay	spend

a About 24% of my income _____ in tax.

b Do you _____ your savings in a high interest account?

c We _____ most of our regular outgoings by direct debit.

d I suppose he _____ about £37,000, with bonuses.

e I need to _____ my overdraft. It's too high.

f They _____ about £300 per month on food.

g We can't _____ to run two cars.

h I'd like to _____ a cheque for £300.

Same as, different from and *similar to*

2 Make comparisons with a partner.

My	situation	is	(very/completely) different from/to	yours.
Our	commitments position outgoings job/company	are	(exactly) the same as (very) similar to	

e.g. – My situation is very different from yours.
  – Why's that?
  – I'm married and you're divorced.
  – It's not so different. For a start, we both have children...

3 READING

Some insurance terms (see page 127)

1 Read the text and answer the questions. What lesson did John and Sally learn?

John and Sally's story

Late last year, our home was broken into and our TV and video were taken. We thought we would make some easy money by adding a few things to our insurance claim. Insurance companies don't check small claims, we thought – but they did, and we had no receipts. A week later, the police caught the thief and he admitted to stealing the television and video, but nothing else. We were interviewed and found out. Insurance evidence helped with the prosecution. We were each fined £200, an expensive lesson for us.

a What happened to John and Sally at the end of last year?

b How did they think they would make some money?

c What happened to the thief a week later?

d What happened to John and Sally?

Reporting a theft

2 In pairs, list valuables that are often stolen. Then practise reporting a theft.

e.g. – Someone has broken into my _____ .
  – Is anything missing?

– Yes, they took my _____ .
– Do you know what it's/they're worth?
– I suppose it's/they're worth about _____ .
– Are you insured?
– Yes, I'll have to make a claim.

4 ACTIVITY

Profit and loss account terms

▲ 'Does this figure represent the total for administrative expenses?'

Half/Twice as much as... (see page 127)

1 Sally Voight is a self-employed media consultant. In pairs, complete her accounts.

Partner A: Your information is below.
Partner B: Your information is on page 128.

Useful language

How much did she spend on [clothing]?
What's the figure for [depreciation]?
What's the figure of [£2,612] for?
What does this figure represent?

SALLY VOIGHT PRODUCTIONS LTD
PROFIT & LOSS ACCOUNT FOR THE YEAR ENDED 31 AUGUST

	Current year	Last year
Turnover (fee income)	163,141	159,244
ADMINISTRATIVE EXPENSES		
Secretarial assistant	15,000	–
Wardrobe / clothing	....	4,477
Travelling, accommodation & subsistence	8,791	13,519
Lighting & heating	1,127	2,281
....	2,612	2,163
Telephone & postage	1,501	3,446
Professional books, journals & subscriptions	....	1,229
Entertainment	2,566	2,620
Photography	....	352
Company registration expenses	25	40
Company pension plan	36,167	....
Director's remuneration & NIC	80,604	97,198
Depreciation	....	300
....	3,100	2,200
Sundry expenses	316	994
Insurance	989	....
Cleaning	920	760
Theatre visits & research expenses	340	105
	159,174	165,365
Operating profit / (loss)	3,967	(6,232)
Interest receivable & similar income	842	....
Interest payable & similar charges	(106)	(377)
Other operating income	–	–
Profit / (loss) on ordinary activities before taxation	4,703	(5,741)
Taxation on ordinary activities	–	–
Profit / (loss) on ordinary activities after taxation	4,703	(5,741)
Balance brought forward	10,561	16,302
Balance carried forward	....	£10,561

2 Comment on the information. Compare the current year of account with the year before. Compare the items of expenditure with your own.

e.g. She spent less/more on _____ this year than last year.
I/We spend about half as much as this.

C Company finances

1 READING

Balance sheet headings

The following explanation of a balance sheet comes from Young & Co's Brewery PLC 1991 Report and Accounts. In pairs, match the headings with the explanations.

shareholders   past profits   current assets/stock   loans
deferred taxation   fixed assets   revaluation reserve   creditors
current assets/debtors

WHAT WE OWN	
Fixed assets	£114,100,416
Current assets:	
Stock	£4,991,097
Debtors	£3,879,715
Cash	£172,247
TOTAL OF WHAT WE OWN	
	£123,143,475
LESS WHAT WE OWE	
Creditors	£8,593,458
Bank	£13,946,871
Loans	£1,800,000
TOTAL OF WHAT WE OWE	
	£24,340,329
Deferred taxation	£2,850,892
Leaving what the company is worth (Book value)	£95,952,254
HOW THE MONEY WAS CREATED	
Shareholders	£7,588,500
Revaluation reserve	£69,590,464
Past profits	£18,773,290
	£95,952,254

a What we need to run a brewery. The brewery buildings, plant, pubs, off-licences and motor vehicles.

b For supplies of malt and hops, wines and spirits. Plus duty, VAT, tax, dividends, services and equipment.

c People who buy shares on the stock exchange, employees as members of the Ram Brewery Trust and other 'B' shareholders.

d What we need to trade. Malt, hops and sugar to make beer. Wine and spirits, spare parts.

e Like a mortgage on a house.

f Surplus on the value of our properties, which goes up over the years in the same way as houses.

g What we are owed by tenants of the pubs, by customers and by others.

h Tax to be paid in the future over many years.

i Money from previous years that has been ploughed back to improve the company.

2 LANGUAGE POINTS

Revise the Passive (see page 129).

1 Make these questions passive. Then supply possible answers.

e.g. When did you complete the accounts?
  <u>When were the accounts completed?</u>
  <u>They were completed last week.</u>

a Have you set targets for the coming year?
_____

b When will you announce the new prices?
_____

c Did they approve the accounts at the AGM?
_____

d How can you measure management performance?
_____

e How much does the company owe?
_____

f Have you transferred the funds yet?
_____

g Where are they going to locate the new plant?
_____

2   Rewrite this statement using Passive forms where possible. Write a similar statement about your company.

> 'The value of the company is currently about $20 million. Last year, we set tough financial targets, which we met without difficulty. In the accounting period to the end of December, we increased profits by more than 15%. We announced these results in January, and the AGM approved the accounts in March. We have established equivalent targets for the current year.'

Common business abbreviations (see page 129)

3   What do the following abbreviations stand for? What others do you know? Work in pairs.

a VAT   d b/f   g RPI   j o/s
b a/c   e IOU   h PC   k PAYE
c AGM   f PTO   i bal   l IT

3 LISTENING

An annual review

▲ 'Our aim is to meet customers' needs profitably.'

1   Listen to the recording, based on an annual review by the Chairman of the British Airport Authority. Number the points in the order they are made.
2   Say something about the key factors which have influenced your business in recent years.

- Retailing revenue per passenger increased by 5.7% over 1990/91.   [ ]
- In the year to the end of March 1992, productivity increased by 6.5%.   [ ]
- Retail expansion will continue with the opening of 90 new shops.   [ ]
- In November, the Civil Aviation Authority announced its new pricing formula.   [ ]
- Staff numbers were reduced and the quality of the service improved.   [ ]
- The new pricing formula sets tough targets for the coming period.   [ ]
- A key factor in these results is the quality of BAA's management team.   [ ]
- BAA increased overall revenue by expanding airport retailing.   [ ]

4 ACTIVITY

Comparing company performance

1   Work with a partner. Find out about his/her company's recent financial performance.
2   Prepare to give a short report on what you have found out.

Profit and loss

| What was your turnover/revenue in _____ ? What were your total sales? How much profit was made? What was the dividend last year? | ◀▶ | Overall revenue increased by _____ over the period _____ . Gross profit rose by _____ . Domestic sales accounted for _____ of our total revenue. |

Balance sheet

| What is the value of your fixed assets? ...and of your current assets/liabilities? How much is owed? What is the total value of the company? | ◀▶ | Net assets are in the region of _____ . Gross liabilities are just over _____ . The company is valued at between _____ and _____ . |

D Payment

1 READING

A request for payment

1 Read the letter. Is this a first, second, or third reminder in your opinion?
2 Write a reply in which you point out that you have already paid the invoice. (There is a sample letter on page 131.)

Dear Mr Petersen,

__INVOICE NO. 3947, DATE 29 JANUARY, AMOUNT £2,175.00__

We do not appear to have received payment of the above invoice, which was due for settlement within twenty-eight days, in accordance with our terms of trading.

If there is any query relating to the amount shown above, please contact us immediately. Otherwise, we would appreciate settlement within the next seven days. If you have paid your account recently, then please ignore this reminder.

Yours sincerely,

D Ashok

Ms D Ashok
Senior Credit Controller

---

2 LANGUAGE POINTS

Unless and *providing/provided* (see page 130)

1 Note the following examples.

We will supply the goods providing/provided we receive a deposit.
We can't supply the goods unless we receive a deposit.

2 Complete the sentences.

a We will take no further action _____ we receive payment within seven days.
b I'll lend you the money _____ you repay me tomorrow.
c They never pay _____ you remind them.
d You can use my office _____ you don't smoke.
e I'll assume everything is OK, _____ I hear from you.
f I can't give you a cheque _____ payment is approved.
g Driving to work saves time _____ you can find parking.
h I'm going to leave _____ I get a salary increase.

Revise the use of prepositions.

3 Complete the sentences.

a Can we pay _____ cheque?
b We'd prefer to be paid _____ cash.
c Interest rates _____ the loan are quite high.
d We're overdrawn _____ the bank.
e I don't understand one of the entries _____ my bank statement.
f What is the rate of the yen _____ the dollar?
g Turnover has increased _____ 15%.
h I think they are _____ debt.

Revise numbers and mathematical terms

4 How would you say the following?

a Let's split the cost 50-50.
b It'll cost between $300-$500.
c What is $5,000 \div 325$?
d What is 5.3×8.7?
e 5,500 Swedish krona + 22½% VAT
f What is $5.004 - 4.346$?
g The tank has a capacity of 60m^3.
h The plant covers an area of 500m^2.
i $^2/_5$ths of our production is exported.
j Bad debts ≈ 3½% of debts o/s.

3 ACCENTS AND PRONUNCIATION

Reasons for not paying

Listen and match the speakers with the reasons for not paying.

a   An Austrian financial controller
b   A New Zealand director of a real estate company
c   An English production manager for a publishing firm
d   A Scottish accountant
e   An Irish export manager

i   There is a query on the sum of money charged.
ii   Payment was in fact made as promised.
iii The invoice was not addressed correctly.
iv   The invoice has possibly got lost in the internal mail.
v   The person who is authorised to make payments is away on business.

4 LISTENING AND ACTIVITY

Requesting payment and giving invoice details

Each and *every* (see page 130)

1   Listen to the phone call between VX Training Manuals and the bought ledger department at Festro Management Systems. Fill in the invoice details.

VX INVOICE

VX TRAINING MANUALS LTD
LONGLEAF WAY
NORTHAMPTON NT4 4MN

DATE OF INVOICE:

INVOICE NUMBER:

DATE PAYABLE:

CHARGE TO: DESPATCH TO:

ORDER REF.	QUANTITY	SBN	TITLE	PRICE
FES/CLE/POS7/6		39832688		
FES/CLE/POS7/6		39833788		

DISCOUNT TERMS:

TOTAL PRICE:

Apparently, it seems that, etc. (see page 130)

▲ 'According to our records, it was paid ten days ago.'

2   Work in pairs. Agree new details for an invoice issued by VX Training Manuals.
Partner A: You are the customer. Call **Partner B** to explain why the invoice has not been paid. Use the phrases below to help you.
Partner B: You work for VX Training Manuals. There are useful phrases for you on page 131.

Useful language

I'm calling in connection with your invoice of _____ .
It seems that it was passed for payment on _____ .
Your cheque should be in the next computer run.
According to our records, it was paid _____ ago.
There was a query on this.
Apparently, the invoice details didn't tie up with our records.
I can't settle it unless payment is authorised.
Didn't you get our letter?

Answers and key phrases, page 130

E Progress check

Complete the gaps in the sentences. In some cases, there is more than one correct answer.

1 Our _____ have increased by 15% in the last year.

   a revenue
   b total sales
   c turnover

2 Our bank _____ is too high.

   a overdraft
   b account
   c statement

3 I notice that £1,000 is still _____ . Could you pay this amount immediately?

   a unpaid
   b outstanding
   c necessary

4 Gross liabilities are _____ $15 million.

   a just over
   b about
   c in the region

5 I'd like to _____ a cheque.

   a pay
   b make
   c cash

6 A lot of money _____ invested last year.

   a was
   b has been
   c is

7 We weren't insured, so we can't put in a _____ .

   a charge
   b claim
   c demand

8 The _____ rate on my overdraft is very high.

   a interest
   b bank
   c loan

9 Expenditure on heating is the _____ as last year.

   a similar
   b different
   c same

10 We will lend you the money _____ you repay us within 30 days.

   a unless
   b providing
   c provided

11 _____ transferred yet?

   a Were the funds
   b Have the funds been
   c Are the funds

12 We normally spend twice as _____ as that on accommodation.

   a more
   b much
   c many

13 We do not appear _____ your payment.

   a receive
   b to receive
   c to have received

14 Could you pay us in _____ , please?

   a dollars
   b cheque
   c cash

15 The company _____ at between 60 and 70 million yen.

   a is worth
   b is valued
   c has current assets

16 Our personal expenditure was down last year, but we _____ spend a lot on clothes.

   a do
   b did
   c didn't

17 We check the balances on the sales ledger _____ two weeks.

   a each
   b every
   c in

18 The decision was taken at the _____ .

   a HQ
   b IOU
   c AGM

PRESENTATIONS

A Introduction

1 CONTENTS

A Introduction
B Preparation
C Facts and figures
D Some company presentations
E Progress check

2 REVISION

1 Revise phrases used in presentations. How would you do the following?

a Welcome people to a presentation.
b Introduce yourself.
c Say what you are going to talk about.
d Invite questions.
e Thank people for listening.

2 Revise the use of *(in order) to*. Complete the examples. What questions might lead to these statements?

a I'm writing (in order) to _____ .
b I'm calling (in order) to _____ .
c We should meet (in order) to _____ .
d They reduced their prices (in order) to _____ .

3 Revise possessive adjectives, possessive pronouns and *whose*. Discuss objects around you.

e.g. Whose is that [briefcase]? Who does that [building] belong to? etc.

4 Revise conjunctions. Then complete the sentence, using the conjunctions below.

We subcontract most of our maintenance work...

a ...because _____ .
b ...and _____ .
c ...although _____ .
d ...but _____ .

5 Revise the use of the infinitive and *-ing* forms. Complete the sentences with the correct form of the verbs in the box.

a Do you need _____ your office?
b Do you enjoy _____ presentations?
c Do you want me _____ you?
d Would you mind _____ the curtains?
e I used _____ speaking to large audiences.

close   give   hate
introduce   phone

6 Check how the following verbs are spelt in the *-ing* form. Then use them in sentences.

be   develop   die   hope   instal   pay
plan   refer   stop   try   use   visit

B Preparation

1 LISTENING

| Checking equipment |

Listen to the telephone call. Tick [✓] the items which the organiser will provide for the speaker's forthcoming presentation.

a flip chart	[　]
an extension lead	[　]
an overhead projector (OHP)	[　]
a slide projector	[　]
a screen	[　]
a whiteboard	[　]
a video recorder (VCR)	[　]
a video camera	[　]
a whiteboard copier	[　]

2 LANGUAGE POINTS

| Verb + preposition + -ing |

1 Complete the sentences with the correct preposition.

a I look forward _____ meeting you again soon.
b Thank you all _____ coming.
c I must apologise _____ starting a little late.
d She's thinking _____ leaving the company.
e He's very good _____ handling difficult questions.
f Are you interested _____ making some money?
g We specialise _____ installing fire prevention equipment.
h Why are you so _____ giving her a job?

| Talking about likes and dislikes |

2 Complete the sentences, using the verbs in the box to help you if necessary.

answer	do	give	have	listen
live	play	speak	work	write

e.g. I'm (not) very keen on <u>speaking in public</u>.
   I much prefer <u>doing business face-to-face to doing it on the phone</u>.

a I don't mind _____
b I (don't) enjoy _____
c I'm fed up with _____
d I can't stand _____
e I'm very fond of _____
f I (absolutely) hate _____
g I love _____
h I sometimes don't feel like _____

| *To be used to* and *to get used to* (see page 132) |

3 Practise *to be/get used to* by writing sentences based on your experience. Then compare notes with a partner.

I'm (not) used to	speaking with/without a microphone.
I can't get used to	using an OHP.
I'll have to get used to	speaking to large groups.
	presenting in English.
	working at weekends.
	not having a secretary.
	being in charge.
	wearing glasses. etc.

e.g. I'm not used to speaking with a microphone. I much prefer speaking to small groups. But I suppose I'll have to get used to it.

3 READING

Preparing notes for a presentation (see page 137)

1 Read the following notes on Siemens AG. Compare them with the full text on page 133.

---

1 Orders
1.1 Orders were up 3% in the period under review.
1.2 While international orders declined, German orders rose by 11%.
1.3 The largest growth was in orders for major systems, particularly in projects to modernise rail and telecommunications systems in East Germany.
1.4 The Automotive Systems group benefited from the increasing use of electronics in cars.

2 Sales
2.1 Worldwide sales rose by 8%.
2.2 Again, the performance was stronger in Germany (14%), but international sales also rose (3%).
2.3 Exports benefited from the high volume of orders received last year.

3 Employees
3.1 The workforce increased by 13,000 owing to the initial consolidation of new companies.
3.2 In some areas, the workforce is being reduced because of insufficient orders and changes in the company's infrastructure.
3.3 Personnel costs rose by 9%.

---

2 In pairs, decide if the notes give a good summary of the original text. Can you improve on them?

3 Write notes for a presentation on your own company or one you know. Refer to the phrases on page 137.

4 ACTIVITY

Final preparations

In pairs, practise preparing for a presentation.

Partner A: You are giving the presentation.
Partner B: You are the training manager. Does **Partner A** have everything he/she needs?

1 Set up the room for the presentation.

Useful language	
How does the OHP work?	Whose is this [mobile phone]?
How do you switch it on?	Shall I put it in my office?
How do you adjust it?	Have you got everything you
Could you get hold of an	need?
extension lead for me?	The OHP bulb needs changing –
I'll need some more marker pens	I'll get a new one.
– these have run out of ink.	Are you planning to use the
	projector?

2 Still in pairs, check that everything is ready.

Useful language	
Is there anything else you need?	We'll begin in five minutes'
Would you like a glass of water?	(time), if you're ready.
How are you feeling?	Shall I introduce you?
I don't mind doing it.	Good luck. I hope it goes well.
I'm not used to speaking	
without an OHP.	

▲ 'I'll need some more marker pens – these have run out of ink.'

C Facts and figures

1 LISTENING

Plotting a graph
Social groups

1 The graph shows the total number of workers unemployed in Britain between 1975 and 1991. Listen to the recording and label the curves that are not identified.

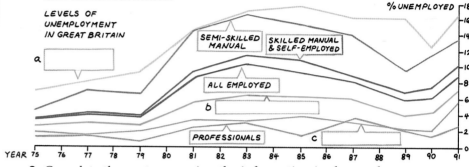

LEVELS OF UNEMPLOYMENT IN GREAT BRITAIN

% UNEMPLOYED

SEMI-SKILLED MANUAL

SKILLED MANUAL & SELF-EMPLOYED

a

ALL EMPLOYED

b

PROFESSIONALS

c

YEAR 75 76 77 78 79 80 81 82 83 84 85 86 87 88 89 90 91

2 Complete the sentences using the information in the graph.

e.g. The graph shows <u>the percentage of unemployed workers</u> in Britain between 1975 and 1991.

a In 1991, the overall rate of unemployment was _____ .

b The level of unemployment among unskilled manual workers fell sharply in _____ .

c The rate of unemployment for professionals peaked at _____ in 1987.

d Among _____ , unemployment rose to over 10% in 1983.

2 ACTIVITY

Describing a graph

▲ 'Sales to Japan have increased dramatically.'

1 Talk about trends and results related to your work, using adjectives and adverbs from the box.

e.g. There was a great improvement in overall performance last year.
Overall, performance greatly improved last year.
There has been a slight rise in sales.
Sales have risen slightly.

> great/greatly   slight/slightly   fast/fast   slow/slowly
> dramatic/dramatically   gradual/gradually   sudden/suddenly
> steady/steadily   sharp/sharply   significant/significantly

2 Present a graph, table or diagram to the rest of the group. The language below may help you.

> **Useful language**
>
> The horizontal axis shows...
> [Sales figures] are shown on the vertical axis.
> [Production levels] reached a peak in...
> At this point on the curve...
> There was a dramatic rise in...
> In [1993], turnover fell sharply.
> In [1992], there was a sudden fall in...
> [Production figures] remained steady during...

3 LANGUAGE POINTS

More numbers

1 In pairs, prepare as many statistics as you can, using the following phrases. Compare your examples with the group.

a one in three/four

b six/seven out of ten

c every 20 seconds/minutes

d every third car/lorry

e between 15 and 20

f three times as much/many

g twice as much/many

h half the quantity/number

Verb + infinitive or *-ing* (see page 134)

2 Compare these sentences. Is there a change of meaning when the infinitive is changed to the gerund, or vice versa?

a Only one in three of our workers likes doing overtime.
Only one in three of our workers likes to do overtime.
b Every twenty seconds, somebody stops to smoke.
Every twenty seconds, somebody stops smoking.
c We saw him giving the presentation.
We saw him give the presentation.
d We began working on this project five years ago.
We began to work on this project five years ago.
e The bulb in the OHP needs changing.
We need to change the bulb in the OHP.
f I don't remember saying that.
I didn't remember to say that.

4 READING

Updating information (see page 134)

Average (see page 134)

Work in pairs.

Partner A: The information you have below is now out-of-date. Contact **Partner B** who has more recent facts and figures.
Partner B: Your information is on page 134.

Marks and Spencer

- There are 291 M&S stores in the UK and the Republic of Ireland.
- St Michael's is the best-selling own label brand in Britain.
- Sales average £517 per square foot.
- The flagship branch at Marble Arch (London) is in the Guinness Book of Records for selling more per square foot than any other shop in Britain.
- It makes a sale every 3.5 seconds.

- This store hands back more money in refunds than the average M&S branch takes.
- It is visited every day by 100,000 people – the capacity of a major stadium.
- It takes delivery of half a million garments every week and has a delivery van of food or textiles arriving every five minutes.
- It sells 5,500 sandwiches a day.
- It sells a ton of fresh and smoked salmon a week.

Source: *The Times*, 8/6/91

---

5 ACTIVITY

Locating information on a page

Present the information on an overhead transparency (or in a text) to the group.

e.g. – This table shows ____ . The figures in the left-hand column are ____ .
– Excuse me, what does the RFT stand for?
– Where is that?
– In the top left-hand corner, just below [the pie chart].

Useful language	
in the top left-hand corner	the second line from the top
in the bottom right-hand corner	the third bullet point
at the top/bottom of the page	the first sentence
on the right-hand side	the final paragraph
in the left-hand column	the blue segment in the pie chart

D Some company presentations

1 LISTENING

> Phrases used in presentations
> (see page 137)

1 Listen to two people presenting information on the same company, Dorm Ltd. Compare the presentations and answer the questions below, putting [1] for the first presenter and [2] for the second presenter.

In your opinion...

a ...which presentation is by the Finance Director of a rival company? [   ]
b ...which one is by the PR Manager of Dorm Ltd? [   ]
c ...which one is made to a board meeting? [   ]
d ...which one is to journalists? [   ]
e ...which one is clearer? [   ]
f ...which one is more interesting? [   ]

2 Which expressions from the list of phrases used in presentations (page 137) do they use?

2 LANGUAGE POINTS

> *Because*, *as* and *since* (see page 135)
>
> *So* and *therefore* (see page 135)

1 Combine the sentences.

a We are running late.	We had to come by train.
b There is no employment in this area.	We need an interpreter. The talk will take place in the boardroom.
c There was a plane strike.	
d He doesn't understand English.	There is no time for more questions. ✓
e The conference room is occupied at that time.	Many people are moving abroad.

a (as) <u>As we are running late, there is no time for more questions.</u>
   (because) _____
b (since) _____
   (therefore) _____
c (so) _____
   (as) _____
d (since) _____
   (so) _____
e (because) _____
   (therefore) _____

> *Although, even though, in spite of (the fact that)*, etc. (see page 135)

2 Change the sentences.

e.g. In spite of the fact that she prepared carefully, her presentation didn't go well.
   (although) <u>Although she prepared carefully, her presentation didn't go well.</u>

a Although it was brand new, the OHP didn't work.
   (in spite of) _____
b We were on time, in spite of the terrible traffic.
   (even though) _____
c He didn't get the job, in spite of having excellent qualifications.
   (but) _____
d I work for the company, but I don't buy their products.
   (although) _____
e Nobody placed an order, even though the presentation was excellent.
   (in spite of) _____
f In spite of the fact that he is nearly 70, he works seven hours a day.
   (even though) _____
g Although he isn't very good at giving demonstrations, he gets excellent sales.
   (in spite of) _____
h They have a limited product range, but their turnover is huge.
   (even though) _____

3 Working in pairs, use the sentences from the previous exercise in short exchanges.

e.g. – How did it go?
– Not very well, although she prepared carefully.

3 READING

Notes on a company's history

1 Read the notes on British Airways. Do they come from a British Airways promotional brochure, or from a newspaper article?

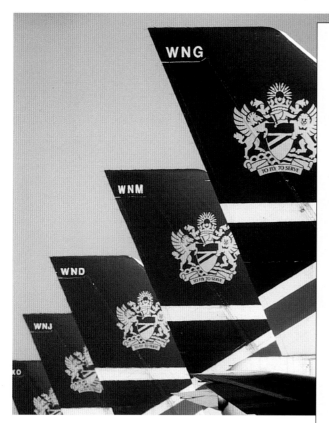
▲ 'In 1992, BA began its global expansion.'

<u>1981</u>	Sir John King arrives at BA, launches survival plan.
<u>1982</u>	BA loses £544m. Laker Airways collapses, anti-trust suit launched.
<u>1983</u>	Colin Marshall appointed chief executive. King is made a life peer.
<u>1984</u>	Richard Branson launches Virgin Atlantic Airways with one jumbo jet.
<u>1985</u>	BA, Pan Am and TWA pay Sir Freddie Laker £8m out of court.
<u>1987</u>	Privatisation at 125p a share (total value £900m).
<u>1988</u>	Takeover of British Caledonian Airways.
<u>1989</u>	Bid to buy into United Airlines, second largest US carrier, fails.
<u>1990</u>	Profits reach record £345m.
<u>1991</u>	Branson accuses BA of 'dirty-tricks campaign'.
<u>1992</u>	BA begins global expansion, buys into airlines in Germany, Australia and France.
<u>1993</u>	BA buys stake in USAir. Apologises to Branson and pays £0.61m in damages and legal costs. King steps down as chairman to become president. Sir Colin Marshall appointed chairman. BA's market value is £2 billion.

2 Find phrases in the text that mean the same as the following.

a resign as
b purchase a part of (a company)
c start/organise
d legal compensation
e a legal case against interference with free trade
f best ever

3 Practise speaking from notes by telling a partner the facts and figures given in the information above, in a more conversational style.

e.g. 'In 1981, Sir John King became head of British Airways. He immediately launched a survival plan...'

4 ACTIVITY

Giving a presentation

1 Prepare a brief presentation on your company or organisation. Refer to the list of phrases used in presentations on page 137.
2 Give your presentation and deal with questions. Refer to tables and charts as necessary.

E Progress check

Complete the sentences. Note that in some cases, there is more than one possible answer.

1 As I _____ earlier, this is the average.

   a told
   b told you
   c mentioned

2 Profits are 5% down _____ last year.

   a for
   b on
   c to

3 If we _____ this chart again, we can compare.

   a look
   b look at
   c look for

4 Could you take a look at _____ , please?

   a the left-hand top corner
   b the left top-hand corner
   c the top left-hand corner

5 I have divided my talk _____ three parts.

   a in
   b into
   c to

6 Did you remember _____ for a projector to be available?

   a asking
   b ask
   c to ask

7 John _____ a few words about our production figures.

   a is going to say
   b is saying
   c is going to talk

8 We have got used _____ with difficult questions.

   a to dealing
   b to deal
   c dealing

9 The OHP didn't work _____ it was brand new.

   a although
   b even though
   c in spite of

10 Would you mind _____ that again?

   a explain
   b to explain
   c explaining

11 _____ we started a little late, I suggest we cut the coffee break.

   a since
   b as
   c so

12 At this point on the _____ , sales go up sharply.

   a line
   b graph
   c curve

13 Could you get hold of a/an _____ lead for me, please?

   a video
   b extension
   c electrical

14 _____ , I must apologise for being late.

   a Firstly
   b Let me start
   c First of all

15 _____ we complete a unit every 5 seconds.

   a In an average day
   b The average
   c On average

16 The vertical _____ shows the rate of unemployment among manual workers.

   a line
   b axis
   c part

17 That _____ to my next point.

   a brings
   b takes
   c brings me

18 Is there _____ you need?

   a anything
   b else
   c anything else

CONTACTS

A Introduction

ANSWERS

2 REVISION

2 a a
  b the
  c –
  d the... the
  e a

4 a so
  b such a
  c such

6 a much
  b many
  c much / a lot
  d many / a lot of
  e a lot of

7 two fifteen, (a) quarter past two, fourteen fifteen, two fifteen p.m., and so on.

INFORMATION

The British telephone alphabet

A for Andrew	D for David
B for Benjamin	E for Edward
C for Charlie	F for Frederick

G for George	Q for Queenie
H for Henry	R for Robert
I for Isaac	S for Sugar
J for Jack	T for Tommie
K for King	U for Uncle
L for Lucy	V for Victory
M for Mary	W for William
N for Nelly	X for Xmas
O for Oliver	Y for Yellow
P for Peter	Z for Zebra

The American telephone alphabet

A for Alba	N for Nan
B for Baker	O for Oboe
C for Charlie	P for Peter
D for Dod	Q for Queen
E for Easy	R for Roger
F for Fox	S for Sugar
G for George	T for Tare
H for How	U for Uncle
I for Item	V for Victor
J for Jig	W for William
K for King	X for X
L for Love	Y for Yoke
M for Mike	Z for Zebra

(Note that we often use other words to represent letters, e.g. A for apple.)

B Contacts at work

KEY PHRASES

Hello, is that Gloria Hay?
Are you busy? Is this a good time?
Go ahead.
It's (It is) about Thursday's meeting.

I'm (I am) tied up at the moment.
Can I call you back this afternoon?
Could I speak to the sales manager?
He's (He is) on another line.   She's not in yet.

We open at 8 am Eastern Standard Time.
That's (That is) eleven o'clock your time.
You're (You are) three hours ahead of us.
It's a public holiday.
  Independence Day   May Day

Can I take a message?
Can you give him a message?
Could you tell him that I called?
Could you ask him to call me?

We need to arrange a time to meet.

Do you know the time of the meeting?
Have you got any time this afternoon?
I have some free time tomorrow.

Have we covered everything?
Is there anything else?
I'm afraid I must go.
I'll (I will) be in touch.
Thank you for calling.
Speak to you soon. (Good)bye.

I often need English in my job.
I can manage in English when we have visitors.
But I sometimes have problems on the phone.

LANGUAGE NOTES

Some uses of *a/an*

Note the following examples of *a/an*.

e.g. A man called for you earlier.
    She is a market researcher.

He was an excellent boss.
It's a European project.
I've had an interesting idea.
Can I take a message?
What a pity!
It cost a thousand dollars.
I'd like a cup of coffee.

Note that if a noun is uncountable or plural, we use *some/any* in place of *a/an*.

e.g. I bought some petrol.
We need some information.
Have you got any change?
She is reading some reports.
Are there any messages for me?
Have you got any time to spare?

Some uses of *the*

Note the following examples of *the*.

e.g. I read the report you sent me.
The government supports the plan.
The people from CIT have arrived.
It's the biggest company in the world.
I'll meet you at the airport.
It's the 21st of July.
Could you tell me the time, please?

Note when *the* is not used.

e.g. Money is very tight right now.
We make shoes for children.
It's Independence Day.
I haven't got time to talk now.
I had lunch with Tom.
He speaks Italian.
She's at home/work.
I came by car.
What rubbish!

Note when *the* is used in names.

e.g. I work for Coca Cola.
I work for the Coca Cola company.
He is head of Finance.
He runs the finance department.
She lives in America.
She lives in the USA.
We are staying at Brown's Hotel.
I have booked a room at the Hilton (Hotel).
Do you have a copy of the *Times*?
Is this the way to Grand Central Station?
How far is it to Heathrow Airport?

Some uses of *some* and *any*

Affirmative:
We need some samples.
We need some stationery.
You could order some.

Negative:
They can't give us any information.
They don't have any leaflets.

We don't need any.

Interrogative:
Have you got some/any biscuits/milk?
Did you ask for some/any?
Where can I get some?

Short answers:
Have you got any spare time?
Yes, I've got some.   No, I haven't got any.
Yes, some.   No, none.

(Note that we do not use the short answer *No, not any*.)

Say, tell and ask

Note these examples of *say, tell* and *ask* in telephone messages.

e.g. Could you say (that) Mary phoned?
(NOT: Could you say him that Mary phoned?*)
Can you tell her (that) I called?
(NOT: Can you tell that I called?*)
Would you ask her to phone me, please?
(NOT: Would you ask to her to phone me, please?*)

ANSWERS

2 LISTENING

2 **a** The factories could improve their service to the sales offices abroad.
b The factory sales offices could operate for a longer period.
c It is 'absolutely essential' that someone in the factory can communicate with the overseas sales company in English.
d It varies from plant to plant, but it is fairly good.

3 LANGUAGE POINTS (suggested answers)

2	a	–		f	any... the
	b	the/a		g	any
	c	an		h	The
	d	–/some/the		i	–/some/the
	e	the		j	a/the

5 LISTENING

1 • not in yet   [✔]
  • having a coffee break   [ ]
  • at lunch   [ ]
  • gone home   [ ]
  • ill or on sick leave   [ ]
  • on holiday   [✔]
  • in a meeting   [✔]
  • with some visitors   [✔]
  • in the building somewhere   [ ]
  • on another number   [✔]
  • away this week   [✔]
  • out at the moment   [ ]
  • not available   [✔]
  • not at his/her desk   [✔]

c Developing contacts

KEY PHRASES

Have you got any contacts in Poland?
Yes, quite a lot.   Yes, a few.
Yes, but not very many.   Yes, but very few.

Do you know anyone who sells photocopiers?
What's (What is) your accountant like?

We've (We have) got a lot of contacts in Eastern
Europe.
I have a few contacts in the tourism business.
I know several people who could help you.
I'm afraid we have very few contacts in that area.

I can recommend the people we use.
They're (They are) very efficient.
He's (He is) reliable and hard-working.
She's good to work with.

Let me give you some names and addresses.
I'll (I will) give you a letter of introduction.

They have such good contacts that it's (it is) difficult
to compete (with them).
Everyone was so helpful that we finished the job in
two days.

We met a couple of days ago.
   the week before last   a week last Friday
I'm (I am) a friend of Rakesh Singh's.

Let's (Let us) meet for lunch on the 10th.
   in ten days' time   a week on Monday
I'll see you then.

LANGUAGE NOTES

Some uses of *much, many, a lot (of)* and *lots (of)*

Affirmative:
There is (quite) a lot of interest in it.
There are (quite) a lot of messages for you.
Many companies are closing down.
There is lots (of work) to do.

Negative:
There isn't (very) much profit in it.
There isn't a lot of profit in it.
We haven't got (very) many competitors.
We haven't got a lot of competitors.
They don't sell much in Turkey.
They don't sell a lot there.

Interrogative:
How much money do you need?
How many pieces would you like?
Have you got much work?
Have you got a lot to do?

Short answers:
Are there many more (calls) to make?

Yes, (quite) a lot.   No, not (very) many.
Yes, lots.   No, not a lot.
Do you like it?
Yes, very much.   No, not (very) much.
Yes, (quite) a lot.   No, not a lot.

Some uses of *a few, a little* and *several*

Note that *a few* and *a little* mean *some*.

e.g. He made (quite) a few phone calls.
      Could I have a little milk, please?

Note that *few* and *little* mean *not many* and *not much*.

e.g. They have (very) few contacts in Poland.
      We have (very) little time.

Note that *several* means more than *some*, but less than *many*.

e.g. We have several contacts in Latin America.
      There are several good watch repairers in the area.
      Several people called for you.

Note the following short answers.

e.g. Have you got any contacts there?
      Yes, several. / Yes, a few. / Yes, but very few.
      Have you got any free time?
      Yes, a little. / Yes, but very little.

So and *such (a)*

Note the following examples of *so*.

e.g. Their products are so cheap that we can't compete.
      Everyone worked so hard that we finished the job
      in two days.
      There are so many points to remember.
      There isn't so much pressure now.

Note the following examples of *such (a)*.

e.g. They have such good contacts that it's difficult to
      compete with them.
      It was such a big order that…
      They have such low prices.
      There's such a lot to do.

Some notes on time references

We use *at* with precise times.

e.g. at midnight
      at two o'clock
      at 4.30

(Note also: at night, at the weekend, at Christmas,
at lunchtime)

We use *on* with days.

e.g. on the 4th of July
      on Monday
      on Independence Day

We use *in* with other times.

e.g. in 1994
in the first quarter
in the morning
in winter

We do not use a preposition with *today, tomorrow, yesterday, tonight,* etc.

e.g. I'll call you tomorrow.

We do not use a preposition with *next, last* and *this*.

e.g. They are coming this Saturday.
I'll see you next week.

ANSWERS

1 READING

1 **a** colleague   **e** branches
b next month   **f** relationships
c responsible for **g** personality
d to lose   **h** confident

2 LANGUAGE POINTS

1 **a** a lot
b much
c a lot of
d many / a lot... a lot
e much
f many / a lot of
g much / a lot... much / a lot

2 (possible answers)
a We have very little time left.
b There are quite a few good restaurants near here.
c We receive very few complaints.
d Would you like a little more?
e There are several possible solutions to the problem.
f There were quite a few people there that I knew.
g We have quite a few contacts in the area.

3 **a** such   **e** so
b so   **f** such a
c such a   **g** such a
d so   **h** so

3 LISTENING

a iv   **b** i   **c** iv   **d** ii

D Outside office hours

KEY PHRASES

I'm (I am) trying to contact Harry Crew.
Do you know how I can get in touch with him?
Is it possible to contact him on this number?
Where can I get hold of him?

I'm meeting him this evening.
We're (We are) going out to dinner.
They're (They are) having a drink together.

The office is closed.
You missed them.   She's (She has) gone home.
I'm afraid we don't (do not) give out private numbers.

Shall I get her to call you in the morning?
Would you like me to get a message to him?
Let me get him to ring you.

Could you give him a message?
Would you ask her to phone me, please?
Would you mind not calling me tomorrow, please?

I've (I have) been trying to contact you.
We didn't (did not) know how to reach you.

It's (It is) good to see you again.
It's good to be here.
I'm glad you made it.

What can I get you?
I'll (I will) have a gin and tonic.
a soft drink   a coffee

Ice and lemon?
Just lemon. No ice.
Help yourself to milk.

ANSWERS

1 READING AND LISTENING

The fax is so urgent because Fiona Temple is meeting Harry Crew for dinner that evening and she doesn't know where.

a One of the security people calls her back.
b No, she doesn't have it.
c They are meeting for a drink at a place called Jason's.
d Harry forgot to fax them to her.
e She will go by taxi.

2 LANGUAGE POINTS

2 (possible answers)
a Could you write this phone number down?
b Would you mind taking this parcel to reception?
c Would you give her a message, please?
d Could you book my flight tickets?
e Would you not give anyone my home number, please.
f Could you not park there, please.
g Would you mind not phoning me tomorrow?

4 (possible answers)
a Could I call you next week?
b Would you like me to prepare an agenda for the meeting?
c Would you like me to get in touch with the Beijing office?
d Shall I book some theatre tickets for you?
e Can I buy you a drink?
f Let me drive you to the station.
g Let me check the order number.

3 LISTENING

1 (possible answers)

TO: Rodney Vale
FROM: June Roach
MESSAGE: Call her at Bowen Tubes between 2 pm and 5 pm tomorrow.

TO: Kjell Peterson
FROM: Tony Conway
MESSAGE: Please send the brochures which you promised – he hasn't received them yet.

TO: Chris
FROM: Bill Tower
MESSAGE: Call him as soon as you get in, on 090 9098, about Mary's visit next week.

TO: The sales manager
FROM: Piero Bellini
MESSAGE: Ring any time this afternoon, on either 34909 (office) or 45690 (mobile).

2 **Dialogue a:** an office
Dialogue b: a bar
Dialogue c: a car hire office
Dialogue d: an exhibition stand

UNIT 2

COMPANIES

A Introduction

ANSWERS

2 REVISION

3 a Everyone is working overtime at the moment.
b Nobody ever goes home before five o'clock.
c She is showing some customers round the factory.
d Two and two make four.

4 faster, fastest; bigger, biggest; more efficient, most efficient; easier, easiest; better, best; worse, worst.

B Your company

KEY PHRASES

What type of company is it?
What are your main activities?
Where are your main markets?

We're (We are) a public limited company.
We make electronic sensors.
We're in the export business.
Our annual turnover is approximately two point five million.
It's (It is) just over three and a half million.
It's more than four and three quarter billion.

The company has three divisions.
Tommy Hoe is the Chief Accountant.
He reports to the Finance Director.
He has a staff of 12 under him.

The company is based in Germany.
It's in the centre of the country.
Our head office isn't (is not) far from Paris.
It's about 70 km east of Brussels.
It's on the coast.
It's outside a village called Hinton.
It's just off the ring road.

The warehouse is beyond the admin block.
My office is on the other side of that building.
The training department is on the third floor.
It's at the end of the corridor.

LANGUAGE NOTES

High numbers

Note the following examples.

e.g. one hundred and fifty thousand (units)
twenty-three million five hundred thousand (dollars)
twenty-three and a half million (dollars)
a/one hundred and twelve point five billion (lire)
half a million (yen)
three quarters of a billion (pounds)
three and three quarter billion (francs)

Note these common abbreviations.

e.g. 9k (nine thousand)
50m (fifty million)
2.5bn (two point five billion)

ANSWERS

2 LANGUAGE POINTS

1 (possible answers)
   a (nought/zero) point two five million dollars
      OR: a quarter of a million dollars
      OR: two hundred and fifty thousand dollars
   b one point two five million pounds
      OR: one and a quarter million pounds
      OR: one million two hundred and fifty thousand pounds
   c (nought/zero) point five million Deutschmarks
      OR: half a million Deutschmarks
      OR: five hundred thousand Deutschmarks
   d three point five million yen
      OR: three and a half million yen
      OR: three million five hundred thousand yen
   e (nought/zero) point seven five billion French francs
      OR: three quarters of a billion French francs
      OR: seven hundred and fifty million French francs
   f three point seven five billion pesetas
      OR: three and three quarter billion pesetas
      OR: three billion seven hundred and fifty million pesetas

2 a employees   d acquisition   g suppliers
  b activities   e subsidiaries   h Sales
  c profit   f clients

3 LISTENING

Complete and return to:
The Manager,
Commercial Banking Services,
National Westminster Bank,
FREEPOST
Hounslow
TW4 5BR.

This information is requested to ensure that future **PHAROS** developments accurately reflect the needs of those using the system. It will not be used for any unrelated mailing activity and will remain absolutely confidential.

For internal use only

1 Name
Title — Ms
First Name — Catherine
Surname — Brass
Position —
Business Name — MASA Partnership
Business Address — 33 Dock Street, London
Postcode — EC4 B70
Telephone Number — 90 897654

2 Type of Business
Sole Proprietor ☐   PLC ☐
Partnership ☑   Subsidiary ☐
Private Limited Company ☐   Other ☐

3 Turnover
Up to £250,000 ☐   £1m-£5m ☐
£250,000-£1m ☑   £5m + ☐

4 Currently involved in import/export
Export only ☐   Import and export ☑
Import only ☐   None ☐

5 Number of companies/divisions
1-2 ☑   3-6 ☐   6+ ☐

6 Number of employees
1-9 ☐   31-100 ☐
10-30 ☑   100+ ☐

7 Is your Company
NatWest Customer ☑   Member of CBI ☐
Ernst & Young Client ☐   Other ☐

8 Please indicate your company's main business activities
Agriculture, forestry and fishing ☐
Energy and water supply ☐
Mining, chemicals ☐
Metal goods, engineering, vehicles ☐
Electronics ☐
Other manufacturing industries ☐
Construction ☐
Retail, distribution, hotels, catering, repairs ☐
Transport, communications ☐
Banking, financial, business services ☑
Education, health, government and local authorities ☐
Other ☐

9 Bankers
NatWest ☑   Barclays ☐   Midland ☐
Lloyds ☐   RBS ☐   Other ☐

10 Disk size required
3½ ☐   5¼ ☑

Copyright in PHAROS is the joint property of National Westminster Bank PLC and Ernst and Young.
You will be licensed to use PHAROS on a single computer only for your internal business purposes, but not for the provision of information or advice to third parties. PHAROS may not be copied, save for any transient copies necessarily created by using PHAROS. You may not modify, de-compile or disassemble PHAROS. PHAROS is supplied "as is" without warranties of any kind. PHAROS is intended as general guidance only. On any specific matter reference should be made to an appropriate professional adviser.

Signed _____
Date _____

C A company profile

KEY PHRASES

What type of company is it?
It's (It is) a power company.
  a gas company   a water company

I believe it's state owned.
I think it's publicly owned.
It's a public utility company.
That means that it's owned by the state.

Is it subsidised?
Although it's a state monopoly, it's run like a private company.

What are your main activities?
Where are your main sites?
How many people do you employ?
Tell me something about your market position.

Basically, we make and distribute electricity.
We run power stations.
  gas works   water works
  sewage plants   coal mines

We are the world's largest producer of electricity.
We account for 94% of the electricity produced in France.

And so what do you do?
I'm (I am) an engineer, but I work as a project manager.
Currently, I'm working in a department called DII.
We make an effort to attract companies who want to do business in France.

INFORMATION

3 LISTENING

A sample company profile

EDF is a public utility company. Its main activities are producing, transporting and delivering electricity in France.
    It has an annual turnover of £15 billion, employs 120,000 people and has 25 million customers. It is a state monopoly.
    Over 20% of the power generated in Europe is produced by EDF. It is a leading exporter of power on the Continent. Although the company is state-owned, it receives no subsidies.

LANGUAGE NOTES

Some expressions of state involvement

It's a publicly owned company.
It's a public utility.

It's a state monopoly.
It's owned by the state/government.
It's subsidised by the state/government.
It's state-subsidised.
It was nationalised/privatised in 1993.

Like and *as*

Note the following examples of *as*.

e.g. As a director, I am responsible.
     She is employed as an engineer.
     This room is used as a storeroom.

Note the following examples of *like*.

e.g. It's run like a private company.
     This model looks just like that one.
     He sleeps like a log.

The Simple Present tense v. the Present Continuous tense

The Simple Present tense:
I work in a power station.
We manufacture electricity.
Do you speak French?
I don't think it's a good idea.
Who owns the company?
I understand you enjoy your work.

The Present Continuous tense:
What are you working on at the moment?
How is business going?
She is learning Arabic.
If you're thinking of relocating, phone us.

ANSWERS

1 READING

  1 EDF is the market leader in France.

  2 **a** nationalised   **c** units
     b exploit   **d** accounted for

2 LISTENING

  1 | | | | |
     |---|---|---|---|
     | Type of company | [✓] | No. of employees | [✓] |
     | History | [✓] | Main sites | [ ] |
     | Main activities | [✓] | Turnover | [ ] |
     | Market position | [✓] | Profit | [ ] |
     | Customer base | [✓] | | |

3 LANGUAGE POINTS (possible answers)

  1 **a** We made a decision on that at yesterday's meeting.
     b They're doing very well with their new product.
     c I'm doing a lot of work for them at the moment.

    d I haven't made any plans yet.
    e We're doing better than QFD in the Middle East.
    f Did they make much money last year?
    g It's a pleasure to do business with you.
    h Are you making notes on this?
    i I have to do some filing before I leave.
    j I'd like to make one point about this.
    k They're doing absolutely nothing about it.
    l He needs to make an effort to get into work on time.

2 a I forget the name of the managing director.
    b It has a turnover of $10m.
    c It is suffering from the effects of recession.
    d It is making a loss. / It makes a loss.
    e What are you doing with the photocopier?

    f I am trying to mend it.
    g If our clients are considering moving, we provide assistance.
    h If companies are thinking of relocating, we give advice.

3 a I believe you rang me this morning.
    b We don't own this equipment.
    c I hear that you're leaving.
    d I can smell fresh paint.
    e I think I know what you're going to say.
    f I know they're interested in this project.
    g I feel that you're making a mistake.
    h That briefcase belongs to me.
    i We are a very small company, which means that we can respond quickly to new developments.

D Competitors

KEY PHRASES

We specialise in mail order.
We're (We are) very active overseas.

We're more profitable than our competitors.
Their prices are less competitive.
They have fewer outlets than us.
Size is the least important factor in this market.

We offer a better service than they do.
The quality of our products is far higher.
Our sales network is much better.
We consider ourselves to be the best in the business.

We're one of the largest producers in North America.
We rank in the top ten companies worldwide.
We have a virtual monopoly.

The competition is very hard.
We face tough competition from South-East Asia.
Our main competitors are having problems.
There isn't (is not) much competition.

They are so strong in the Middle East that we can't (cannot) compete with them.
We can't compete on price.
Their wage costs are lower.

I don't (do not) think that's (that is) true.
What's your view?
I agree with you.

LANGUAGE NOTES

Comparative and superlative adjectives

Short adjectives:
short, shorter, shortest
large, larger, largest
big, bigger, biggest

Longer adjectives:
expensive, more expensive, most expensive
    less expensive, least expensive

Irregular adjectives:
good, better, best
bad, worse, worst
far, farther (further), farthest (furthest)
little, less, least
much, more, most

Examples:
Their subsidy is (much) larger than ours.
It's (far) more profitable than it was.
It's (not) the most important development.
It's the best alternative.
This job is (much) less interesting than my last one.
Size is the least important factor in this market.
We're (not) as well established as you are.

ANSWERS

1 READING

  2 knowhow   interests
      guarantees turnover
      employing emphasised
      increases   collaboration

2 LANGUAGE POINTS

  2 Company A [1]   Company D [4]
      Company B [3]   Company E [6]
      Company C [2]   Company F [5]

  3 (possible answers)
  a Bulgaria, Czech Republic, Hungary, Russia, etc.
  b Argentina, Bolivia, Brazil, Chile, Colombia, etc.
  c China, Japan, North Korea, South Korea, etc.

d Algeria, Egypt, Libya, Morocco, Tunisia, etc.
e Iran, Iraq, Israel, Jordan, Saudi Arabia, Syria, etc.
f Belize, Costa Rica, El Salvador, Guatemala, etc.
g China, Japan, Taiwan, Thailand, Vietnam, etc.

4 LISTENING

a iii b v c i d ii e iv

UNIT 3

PERSONNEL

A Introduction

ANSWERS

2 REVISION

6 (possible answers)
a sitting-room, dining-room, bathroom, toilet, hall, stairs, landing, main bedroom, children's bedroom
b conference room, meetings room, sales office, reception, storeroom, lift, canteen, kitchen

B Personal background

KEY PHRASES

I was born in the south of Spain.
Where do you live now?
We have a house on the other side of town.
It's (It is) a terraced house.

Are you married?
I have three children.
They're (They are) still at school.
The oldest is 14.

What are you doing these days?
Are you still in the food industry?
How long have you been self-employed?
I'm (I am) not working full-time.
I'm in part-time employment.

Have you ever had to cancel a holiday?
Have you ever had to fire someone?
No, never.   Yes, a long time ago.

What do you do in your free time?
I spend most of my time gardening.
I'm not very keen on reading.

And how have you been?
How is your wife?
I've had a bad back.

Her eye trouble is much better.
We both suffer from hayfever.

What are you up to these days?
Do you still work for DBS?
I'm still working with John.
Hasn't he retired yet?

LANGUAGE NOTES

The Present Perfect tense

Affirmative:
I have (I've) finished the job.
He has (He's) resigned.

Negative:
I have not (haven't) decided yet.
She has not (hasn't) changed her mind.

Interrogative:
What have you done about...?
Has he finished the work yet?

Short answers:
Yes, I have. No, I haven't.
Yes, he has. No, he hasn't.

Examples:

We have been here an hour (and we're still waiting).
I have been a sales rep all my life.
Have you done this sort of work before?
They've never been to Egypt.
The President has announced his resignation.
The situation hasn't changed much since yesterday.

Some examples of *have got to* and *have/had to*

Present:

I often have to speak English on the phone.
Do you ever have to work on Saturdays?
He doesn't have to reply till tomorrow.
I have got to call my office.
We have got to improve our security.

Past:

I often had to speak French with customers.
I had to phone my wife.
We had to change our suppliers.
Did you ever have to work at night?
He didn't have to pay the full price.

ANSWERS

1 ACTIVITY (possible answers)

Do you still live there?
Where do you live now?
Do you live in a house or a flat?
Are you married?
Do you have any children?
Are they boys or girls?
How old are they?
Where did you go to school/college/university?
What do you (like to) do in your free time?

2 LISTENING

They know each other fairly well, but they haven't met for a long time.

(vocabulary relating to main speaker)
made redundant
collecting antiques
reading
walking
bungalow

3 LANGUAGE POINT

1 (possible answers)
a Have you ever played badminton?
b How long have you lived in the house you have now?
c Profit has fallen in the last quarter.
d The Managing Director has retired.
e We have just met two colleagues of yours.
f They haven't called me yet.
g He still hasn't made his mind up.

4 READING (possible answers)

1 The advertisement is for the Clerical Medical Investment Group, an insurance company in the UK.

2 a Have you ever been stuck in Stuttgart?
b Have you ever missed the last shuttle home?
c Have you ever had to sit through a sales conference?
d Have you ever had to be nice to a smart-ass?
e Have you ever had to cancel a holiday?
f Have you ever had to have 'one last drink' with a client?
g Have you ever had to m-m-make a speech?
h Have you ever worked so late you've slept in the office?
i Have you ever been stuck in a suit when it's 80° in the shade?
j Have you ever had to catch the 7 am shuttle?
k Have you ever had to fire someone?
l Have you ever been misquoted by a trade journalist?

C Conditions of work

KEY PHRASES

What fringe benefits do you receive?
What perks do you get?

Do you get private health insurance?
Does your company pay your phone bill?
Is there a bonus scheme?
What's (What is) it worth?

Is your office pleasant to work in?
What's it like to work in?

Is there enough space for everyone?
Is the lighting bright enough for you to read comfortably?

There's (There is) plenty of space.
The lighting is adequate.
All the seats are adjustable.

The work surfaces are too small to work on.
The shelves are too high for me to reach.

Where were you working this time last year?

What were you working on?
What were you doing between three and four?

We were having a cup of coffee when the fire started.
I was coming down in the lift when the alarm went off.

When I got outside, smoke was coming out of the window.

I'd (I had) just finished work.
I tried to call you, but you had gone home.

INFORMATION

4 ACTIVITY

Partner B's information:

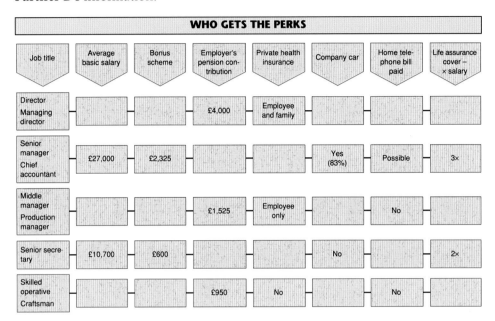

Job title	Average basic salary	Bonus scheme	Employer's pension contribution	Private health insurance	Company car	Home telephone bill paid	Life assurance cover – × salary
Director / Managing director			£4,000	Employee and family			
Senior manager / Chief accountant	£27,000	£2,325			Yes (83%)	Possible	3×
Middle manager / Production manager			£1,525	Employee only		No	
Senior secretary	£10,700	£600				No	2×
Skilled operative / Craftsman			£950	No		No	

WHO GETS THE PERKS

Useful Language

What is a [managing director's] basic salary?
Does he or she get private health insurance?
What does it cover?
Does the company pay his/her phone bill?
Is there a bonus scheme?
What is it worth?

LANGUAGE NOTES

Too and *enough*

Note the following examples of *too*.

e.g. This equipment is too heavy for me to lift.
Is the noise too loud for you?
These shelves are too high to reach.
The light is bright, but it isn't too bright.
She speaks too quickly for me to understand.

Note the following examples of *enough*.

e.g. Is the room cool enough to work in comfortably?
There isn't enough space for us all to work comfortably.
Have you got enough chairs for everyone?
Is the software straightforward enough for me to use?
I didn't read the instructions carefully enough.

The Past Perfect tense

Affirmative:
We had (We'd) gone home by then.
She had (She'd) already told us that...

Negative:
I had not (hadn't) expected the job to be...
They had not (hadn't) started when...

Interrogative:
Had the meeting ended by the time you...?
Had I begun my new job...?

Short answers:
Yes, it had.   No, it hadn't.
Yes, you had.   No, you hadn't.

Examples:
I thought that you'd made a decision.
When I went down to reception, the visitor had already left.
Had we moved to the new offices when you joined the company?
They'd just finished work when the alarm went off.
I hadn't done anything like that before.

The Past Continuous tense

Affirmative:
I was waiting for you to call.
We were discussing that problem.

Negative:
It was not (wasn't) working.
You were not (weren't) listening.

Interrogative:
What was he saying?
Were you expecting me?

Short answers:
Yes, I was.   No, I wasn't.
Yes, we were.   No, we weren't.

Examples:
They were interviewing someone when you phoned.
I was reading my notes while he was talking.
It's OK, we weren't doing anything special.
Where were you working this time last year?

ANSWERS

1 READING

1 a	7	e	9
b	8	f	3
c	2	g	10
d	1	h	5

i	4	l	11
j	6	m	12
k	14	n	13

2 LANGUAGE POINT

a asked (had asked)
b had arranged
c called
d had tried
e was not (had not been)
f did not know (had not known)
g wanted
h had left

3 LISTENING

2 [ ] Sofia Fallon had gone home.
  [✓] Sheila Kite was having a cup of coffee.
  [✓] Andrew Syrah was putting on his coat.
  [✓] Steven Upton was coming down in the lift.

D Job descriptions

KEY PHRASES

She's (She is) a qualified accountant.
She trained as an accountant with Touche Ross.
He studied law at university.
He has a degree in business studies.

He's (He is) responsible for the day-to-day running of the department.
He has to liaise with the production manager.
She spends a lot of her time advising people.
She doesn't (does not) have much to do with the sales side.
It isn't (is not) her job to do the typing.

What's (What is) she like?
She's honest and reliable.
  dishonest   unreliable

What does she look like?
She's quite tall with straight blond hair.
She's wearing a silk blouse and a short, black skirt.
He has dark, curly hair.
He's wearing a pin-striped suit and a spotted tie.

I wish he wouldn't (would not) wear that tie.
It's (It is) too bright.
I don't (do not) think she should wear that skirt.
It's too short.

Can I make a suggestion?
You should change your jacket.

You don't agree, do you?
No, I don't.

LANGUAGE NOTES

Replying to negative statements

Note the following examples.

You don't agree with me.
To confirm: No, I don't.
To deny: Yes, I do.

She didn't phone.
To confirm: No, she didn't.
To deny: Yes, she did.

They didn't give you the job.
To confirm: No, they didn't.
To deny: Yes, they did.

This isn't your signature.
To confirm: No, it isn't.
To deny: Yes, it is.

Some adjectives to describe appearance and dress

Some common materials:
cotton, leather, silk, wool, denim, corduroy, nylon, acrylic, lycra, polyester

Some common designs:
floral, plain, spotted, striped, checked

Some adjectives describing colours:
bright, dark, light, pastel, pale

Some adjectives describing hair:
blond, fair, grey, dark, curly, wavy, straight, short,
thinning

Forming the opposites of adjectives

Un- is the most common negative prefix.

e.g. profitable/unprofitable
       safe/unsafe

In- is another common negative prefix. It becomes *im-*
before an *m* or *p*; *ir-* before an *r*; and *il-* before an *l*.

e.g. direct/indirect
       flexible/inflexible
       possible/impossible
       mobile/immobile
       legal/illegal
       relevant/irrelevant

Dis- is another common negative prefix.

e.g. honest/dishonest
       organised/disorganised
       encouraging/discouraging (NOT: disencouraging*)

-Less is a common negative suffix.

e.g. colourful/colourless

Wish

Note the following examples of *wish*.

e.g. I wish you wouldn't wear that suit.
       I wish she could speak Cantonese.
       I wish we could go by car.
       I wish they didn't smoke.
       I wish he wasn't so untidy.
       I wish it was Tuesday.

ANSWERS

1 READING

2 **a** She mainly works with corporate clients, and
local and central government.
  b She spends most of her time advising clients
on how best to implement environmental
management systems.
  c Her most recent job was a project to reduce
levels of carbon dioxide in Zimbabwe.
  d Her next project is in Romania.
  e She left university in 1986.

2 LISTENING (possible answers)

a She is secretary to the production director.

b The job involves keeping his diary, typing,
sending memos, arranging meetings, keeping the
files straight, arranging lunch appointments, and
arranging travel.
c She has dealings with the factory floor when a
machine has broken/failed and needs repairing;
she also liaises to check on progress.
d She doesn't think it is very good.
e She has been with the company for ten years.
f No, she began as a clerk in the maintenance
department. She became secretary to her boss
when he was the works manager, before he was
promoted to production director.
g She goes out for meals, or to the pub, or she sees
friends.
h No, she doesn't. Once a year, there is a dinner-
dance, which she attends, and that is about all.

3 LANGUAGE POINTS

1 **a** No, I don't.
  b No, they haven't.
  c No, I can't.
  d No, they didn't.
  e No, I wouldn't.

2 quite tall   [F]
   slim   [F]
   has straight blond hair   [T]
   is wearing a short skirt   [T]
            a silk blouse   [?]
            woolly tights   [F]
            high-heeled shoes   [T]

3 (possible answers)
   quite tall
   medium build
   has short dark hair
   wears glasses
   is wearing a pin-striped suit
            a white shirt
            a tie
            black lace-up shoes

4 noisy   unreliable
   honest   promising
   selfish   tolerant
   unpleasant   unintelligent, stupid
   thoughtful   impolite, rude
   unattractive, ugly careless
   lazy   disorganised
   inefficient

PRODUCTS

A Introduction

ANSWERS

2 REVISION

1. one thousand two hundred and fifty
   one point two five
   a/one hundred and fifty dollars
   the twelfth of the fourth, (nineteen) ninety-three
   one and three quarters
   twelve point five per cent
   a hundred and twenty-five thousand pounds
   the first of the twelfth, (nineteen) sixty-two

2. fifteen grams
   a/one hundred and seventy-five pounds
   five metres by eight metres
   two point five centimetres
   a/one hundred kilometres per/an hour
   twenty-one degrees Celsius/Centigrade

3. (possible answers)
   metal: steel, silver

man-made: plastic, glass, paper, polystyrene, nylon
natural: wood, cotton, rubber, leather, wool

4. a did you call
   b Have you called
   c Did you call
   d was
   e Have you ever been

5. (possible answers)
   a big, new car
   an old, wooden chair
   a wonderful, cold drink
   a grey, metal box
   an interesting, French film
   a hot, sunny day

6. a The company who we are talking about is... [ ]
   b The people which we are training are... [ ]
   c The organisation we are joining is... [✔]
   d The prices that we are charging are... [✔]
   e The products which we are launching are... [✔]

B The products you make/use

KEY PHRASES

Our products are reasonably priced.
   extremely well-made
   highly competitive

What are they made of?
The casing is plastic.
The working parts are stainless steel.
They are 25% rubber.
It's (It is) made of concrete.
It covers an area of 14 square metres.

25% equals a quarter.
66.6% equals two thirds.

We stock the full product range.
All items are available from stock.
Delivery takes two days.
The reference number is 12/473-AZ9.

I'd like to order one.
Do you still supply them in green?
We don't stock that colour any more.
That line is discontinued.
We used to make them in that size.
We used to stock that design.
It used to be very popular, but there's (there is) no longer any demand.

What is the nearest equivalent?
The A444-909 is very similar.

INFORMATION

4 ACTIVITY

Partner B's information:

Useful language
We don't stock that size/colour/design any more. We used to supply them, but that line is now discontinued. We no longer make them in that colour. The A444-909 is very similar.

Catalogue no: A444-908. No longer available.
Nearest equivalent
Catalogue no: A444-909
Solid brass frame, white dial, bold black Arabic numerals, quartz movement.
Diameter: 240mm (9½″)
£55

Catalogue no: A444-911. Line discontinued.
Nearest equivalent
Catalogue no: A444-912
Quartz movement, black frame, silver dial.
Diameter: 330mm (13″)
£40

Catalogue no: A490-89. Unlimited stocks available.
Battery-operated round quartz wall clock. Red case with easy-to-read graphics and non-scratch glass.
Diameter: 229mm (9″)
£25

LANGUAGE NOTES

Adverbs in phrases

We can use adverbs to modify adjectives.

e.g. absolutely accurate, really expensive, completely reliable

We can use adverbs to modify past participles.

e.g. extremely well-made, highly recommended, beautifully designed

Numbers and symbols

Reference numbers:

106/B-2	one oh six stroke B dash two
A3/077-PP	A three slash zero seven seven hyphen double P

Dimensions:

10m x 6.5m	ten by six point five metres
10m x 10m	ten metres square
10m²	ten square metres
10m³	ten cubic metres

Fractions:

$^2/_3$	two thirds
$^3/_4$	three quarters
$^1/_{12}$	a/one twelfth
$^3/_8 = 37.5\%$	three eighths equals thirty-seven point five per cent

Some materials and metals

Some common metals:
aluminium, chrome, copper, iron, steel, brass, silver, gold

Other common materials:
concrete, brick, glass, plastic, stone, wood, quartz, rubber, cardboard, polystyrene

Used to

Affirmative:
You used to stock wall clocks.
They used to be our best line.

Negative:
We didn't (did not) use to advertise.
Nobody used to buy them.

Interrogative:
Where did you use to get them?
Did they use to sell well?
Did we use to supply many?

Short answers:
Yes, they did.   No, they didn't.
Yes, we did.   No, we didn't.

Examples:
I used to work in credit control.
That line didn't use to be very popular.
We never used to get any complaints.
Did you use to make them in a larger size?

ANSWERS

1 LISTENING

　1 a ii   **b** iv   **c** iii   **d** i

2 LANGUAGE POINTS (possible answers)

　1 a one two slash four seven three four hyphen A Z nine seven
　　OR: twelve stroke four seven three four dash A Z ninety-seven
　b one seven dash V L D slash double four slash nine double nought
　　OR: one seven hyphen V L D stroke four four stroke nine zero zero
　　OR: seventeen dash V L D slash forty-four slash nine hundred
　c three eighths
　d a/one tenth
　e fourteen square metres
　f thirty-seven cubic centimetres

g twenty-five per cent equals one quarter
h sixty-six point six per cent equals two thirds

2 a steel, wood
b glass, plastic
c concrete, iron
d bricks, cement

e wool, silk
f canvas, leather
g wood, glue
h bread, butter

3 READING AND LISTENING (suggested answers)

1 The sales manager expresses his interest in the opportunity to become a supplier for SM Electrics, and he sends the information they require.

a SM Electrics' main market is Australia.
b RG Holdsworth recommended RA Plastics.
c Andrea Soleman needs details of the product range, price lists, and delivery terms.
d She needs it by June 20th because she will be finalising the company's plans to visit prospective suppliers by that date.

2 A car will pick Andrea Soleman up from the Centre Hotel at 12.00 the next day and take her to RA Plastics. Tony Pang Wan will take her out to lunch.

C Product descriptions

KEY PHRASES

How long have you been making balloons?
For about 20 years.
We've (We have) been selling this model since 1979.

We're (We are) the largest manufacturer of balloons in the world.
On average, we build one every day.
No other manufacturer can match our experience.

The Viva models are particularly suitable for beginners.
They range in size from 590 cubic metres to 2,550 cubic metres.
That's (That is) 90,000 cubic feet.

We have off-the-shelf packages.
These are available at the lowest possible prices.
They come in a range of colours and trims.
There are various options.

I'd (I would) like a round one.
This one's (one is) L-shaped.
That one's in the shape of a cross.

First, the fabric is cut into panels.
Then it's (it is) sewn together.
At this stage, it's reinforced.
Finally, it's connected to the frame.

Could you tell me if this model is suitable?
Do you know whether they run on petrol?
I'd like to know how often they need servicing.

LANGUAGE NOTES

Some imperial measurements

1 foot = 0.305 metres
1 mile = 1.609 kilometres
1 ounce = 28.35 grams
1 pound = 0.454 kilograms
1 pint = 0.568 litres
1 gallon = 4.54 litres

The Present Perfect Continuous tense

Affirmative:
I have been waiting for an hour.
It has been raining since this morning.

Negative:
They haven't (have not) been listening.
It hasn't (has not) been selling well.

Interrogative:
What have you been doing all morning?
Has he been talking about this for long?
Have you been travelling since yesterday?

Short answers:
Yes, he has.   No, he hasn't.
Yes, we have. No, we haven't.

Examples:
How long have you been producing this line?
We've been marketing this product since 1983.
We haven't been receiving your faxes.
I've been trying to get through for half an hour.

Indirect questions

Note the following examples of questions.

e.g. Can/Could you tell me if you have it in stock?
Do you know when they'll be ready?
I'd like to know how much it is.

Note the following examples of responses to indirect questions.

e.g. I don't know whether we have them in stock.
I'm not sure when they'll be ready.
I'll have to check how much it is.

The Simple Present Passive tense

Affirmative:
I'm (I am) employed by...
The two sheets are stapled together.

Negative:
Normally, he isn't (is not) consulted.
We aren't (are not) contacted until...

Interrogative:
Is it manufactured locally?
Are they sewn together?

Short answers:

Yes, it is.   No, it isn't.
Yes, they are.   No, they aren't.

Examples:
Are you invited to those meetings?
It isn't handled by this department.
The sections are painted by hand.
The nylon is cut into panels.

ANSWERS

1 READING

No, it doesn't.

a	T	**c**	F	**e**	T	**g**	T
b	?	**d**	F	**f**	T		

2 LANGUAGE POINTS

2 **a** He has never met the MD.
   He has been working for the company for 11 years.
 b They have been making hang-gliders since 1984.
   They have produced over 3000 hang-gliders in that time.
 c I have been calling clients all morning.
   I have only spoken to five so far.
 d It has rained three times this week.
   It has been raining all day today.

3 (possible answers)
a I'd like to know how big it is.
b Can you tell me if/whether it runs on petrol or gas?
c Do you know how often it needs servicing?
d I'd like to know where I can buy it.
e Could you tell me if/whether you can deliver it on Friday?
f Do you know how soon you can arrange delivery?

4	**a** a wheel	**e** a cigarette packet
	b a chess board	**f** a shield
	c a rugby ball	**g** a golf club
	d a pyramid	**h** a plus sign

3 LISTENING

1 b   2 d   3 a   4 c

D Compliments and complaints

KEY PHRASES

I'd (I would) like to make a complaint about a faulty, plastic smoke alarm.
   this new, fibreglass tennis racket

There are some things which need sorting out.
There are some parts that need mending.

The windows don't (do not) close properly.
The light doesn't (does not) work.
There is something wrong with it.
And it is scratched.
   broken   dented   cracked

We're (We are) very unhappy about it.
It isn't (is not) good enough.

We're sorry to hear that.
We're very sorry about it.
That's (That is) extremely unfortunate.
We apologise for any inconvenience.
What can we do to put it right?

I spoke to the man that wrote the report.
I contacted the customer who made the complaint.
I'll (I will) phone the person whose job it is.

He's (He is) very pleased with it.
He says it's (it has) been working very well indeed.
They haven't (have not) had any trouble with it since they bought it.

That's good to hear.
Thank you for saying that.

LANGUAGE NOTES

Some notes on relative pronouns

Note when we use *who* or *that*.

e.g. the engineers who/that serviced it
   the woman who/that made the complaint

Note when we use *which* or *that*.

e.g. a product which/that sells well
   a company which/that makes pharmaceuticals

Note when we can omit *who/which/that*.

e.g. the salesman (who/that) I spoke to
   the advertisement (which/that) I saw

Note when we use *where*.

e.g. the town where the factory is
the office where I work

Note when we use *whose*.

e.g. employees whose work is satisfactory
a firm whose main market is Korea

The order of adjectives

Note the following examples.

e.g. a large, red container
a small, rectangular table
a white, polystyrene box
a long, Tibetan jacket
black, leather golfing shoes
a faulty, plastic smoke alarm
a new, fibreglass tennis racket

INFORMATION

1 READING

Sample letter:

• WEX WHOLESALERS •
10 Pole Road
Manchester MC5 44W

Dear Sir/Madam,

As stockists of PX alarms, we are writing to complain
about your XC-4 model. There seems to be a fault in
this product. Recently, we have received a number of
complaints from customers, who say that the alarm
sometimes goes off for no apparent reason. It has also
failed to go off in the presence of smoke.

Clearly, the situation must be corrected as soon as
possible. May we suggest that you issue a recall
notice in the press?

Could you also please remove our existing stock of
the XC-4. We are prepared to accept your XC-3 model
in replacement.

Yours faithfully,

Rex Cuthbert

Rex Cuthbert
Purchasing Manager

ANSWERS

1 READING

1 The notice has been issued because PX Alarms
has discovered a fault in their XC-4 range of
smoke alarms.

a F   **b** T   **c** F   **d** ?

3 LISTENING

paintwork: scratched
bumper: loose
petrol tank: leaking
headlamp: doesn't work
windows: stiff
petrol gauge: broken

4 LANGUAGE POINTS

1 **a** This is the woman whose car was damaged.
b The hotel where I stayed is expensive.
OR: The hotel (which/that) I stayed in is
expensive.
c I wrote down the fax number (which/that) he
gave me.
d Have you found that file (which/that) you lost
yesterday?
e I drove to Leoton where we have a warehouse.
f The man who works in the office next to mine
is very helpful.
g I work for a Taiwanese company which/that
manufactures electronic toys.
h That's the man whose job it is to deal with
these enquiries.

2 (possible answers)
a grey, Japanese answerphone
a cheap, plastic smoke alarm
an efficient, German photocopying machine
a new, square, black desk

SERVICES

A Introduction

ANSWERS

2 REVISION

2 (possible answers)
a I may go to Hong Kong this week.
b I ought to ring my boss before the weekend.
c I should write a report on the conference, but I don't have time.
d I couldn't park outside, because there weren't any parking spaces left.
e We need to replace this machine because it's getting old.
f I would learn Russian, but people tell me it's difficult.

3 (possible answers)
a They don't have to wear a company tie.
b I must call my wife.
c I mustn't be late tomorrow.
d You have to drive on the right here.
e We must meet for lunch some time.

4 a himself   c ourselves
  b myself   d herself

5 a I <u>am</u> sorry.
  b I'm <u>so</u> sorry.
  c I'm <u>very</u> sorry.
  d I'm very sorry in<u>deed</u>.
  e I'd <u>like</u> to a<u>po</u>logise.
  f <u>Please</u> accept my apologies.

B The services you provide/use

KEY PHRASES

We handle the cleaning ourselves.
We handle our own cleaning.
We handle it in-house.
We subcontract the catering to CLK.
Routine maintenance work is done by an outside contractor.

They offer an excellent service.
The service they provide is very good value.

We ought to have the system updated.
We need to have the part serviced.
We must get the machine replaced.

We're (We are) considering whether to lease or to buy.
What's (What is) the cost of outright purchase?
What does it cost to lease?

There's (There is) a discount of 20%.
There's a 20% discount.
The net figure is £1512.
VAT is on top.

The rental is £9.50 per week.
  per week   weekly
  per month   monthly

We offer a full service contract.
What does the maintenance contract include?
It covers routine and emergency call-outs.
It doesn't (does not) cover spare parts.
The service charge is £190 per annum.
The first six months is free of charge.

INFORMATION

1 ACTIVITY

Partner B: You are interested in using an F20 facsimile machine. Before you make a decision, ask **Partner A** about the following points:

• the cost to lease over five years;
• the cost to lease over three years;
• the cost to buy outright.

Find out about discounts, VAT and service charges. What does the maintenance contract include/exclude?

LANGUAGE NOTES

Payment times

Note the following examples.

e.g. The rental is £9.50 a day.
    It has to be paid monthly.
    We are invoiced quarterly.
    They charge £1000 per quarter.
    She earns $50,000 per year.
    The service charge is reviewed every six months.

Note the following abbreviations.

p.a. = *per annum* (Latin), per year, annually
p.d. = per day, daily
p.w. = per week, weekly

To have/get something done

Note the following examples.

e.g. We should get some photographs taken.
We had the photocopier replaced.
We must get that machine repaired.
We ought to have the system updated.
Where can I get this machine serviced?
Where can I have my suit cleaned?

Expressing necessity

Note the following examples.

e.g. We ought to have the machine serviced.
You should check the contract.
We need to get a new part.
I have to replace the damaged equipment.
You must inform the tax authorities.

ANSWERS

2 LISTENING

1

Service	Speaker (a-d)	P/U	Reason for use
express parcel delivery	d	U	speed / insurance cover
emergency breakdown	b	P	good reputation / short waiting time
site maintenance	c	U	the cheapest option / a time-saving strategy
creche	a	U	friendly staff / good value

3 LANGUAGE POINTS (possible answers)

1 a We must have/get them painted.
  b We (will) have to have/get it repaired.
  c I need to have/get them replaced/changed.
  d We ought to have/get it updated.
  e I must have/get it changed/replaced.
  f We should have/get them serviced.

4 ACCENTS AND PRONUNCIATION

	catering	security	cleaning	language training
A Senegalese technical programme officer	SC	SC	IH	–
A Chilean office clerk	IH	SC	–	SC
An Irish export manager	SC	IH	SC	–
A Dutch customer services manager	SC	–	SC	IH
A Scottish sales executive	SC	–	–	SC

C Dealing with problems

KEY PHRASES

We regret that we've (we have) had to cancel the course due to insufficient demand.
  because of financial difficulties
  as a result of complaints by customers

We've just heard that the delivery hasn't (has not) arrived.
As far as I know, they haven't (have not) received it yet.
It should have arrived by now.
We're (We are) very worried about the situation.

That's (That is) strange, it was despatched on Monday.
I've (I have) checked with the driver.
He says that he delivered it on Tuesday.
Apparently, Mr North signed for it.

We apologise for any inconvenience which this might have caused.
We'd (We would) like to apologise for not coming to the meeting.

Please accept our apologies.

I'm (I am) sorry, but it just isn't (is not) good enough.
You should have let us know sooner.
You ought to have made the situation clear.
You could have sent us a fax.
We understand your position, but please make sure that it doesn't (does not) happen again.

Don't (Do not) worry, it really doesn't matter.
Please don't apologise, it was no trouble.
There is really no need to apologise.

LANGUAGE NOTES

Due to, on account of, etc.

Note the following examples.

e.g. The power failed because of an electrical fault.
All flights are delayed due to bad weather.

We had to cancel the deal on account of problems with our suppliers.
As a result of complaints from customers, we have had to recall batch 673/A.

The Past tense of modal verbs

The modal verbs are *can, could, may, might, must, ought to, have to, shall, should, will* and *would*.

Affirmative:
He must have forgotten.
They may have left already.

Negative:
He won't (will not) have gone yet.
I shouldn't (should not) have mentioned it.

Interrogative:
Who can have called?
Would you have accepted...?
Might he have done it?

Short answers:
Yes, I would.   No, I wouldn't.
Yes, he might.   (No, he wouldn't.)

(**Note:** The short answer *No, he mightn't* is not possible.)

Examples:
The delivery should have arrived by now.
You ought to have made the situation clear.
You could have sent us a fax instead.
He may have lost the address.
We apologise for any inconvenience which this might have caused you.

Some examples of apologies

Making apologies:
I'm very sorry to have to interrupt you, but...
I'm sorry (that) I didn't call earlier.
I'm very sorry indeed about the delay.
We'd like to apologise for not finishing on time.
We do apologise for any problems this might cause you.

Please accept our apologies.

Accepting apologies:
That's OK. / Not at all. / Don't worry.
It's no problem. / Never mind.
It really doesn't matter.
Please don't apologise.
There's really no need to apologise.

Rejecting apologies:
Why didn't you tell me earlier?
You should have let us know.
You ought to have made the situation clear.
I'm sorry, but it just isn't good enough.
Please make sure that it doesn't happen again.

ANSWERS

2 LANGUAGE POINTS

1 a I must have left them in the office.
   b You could have sent me a fax.
   c You should have checked with me first.
   d She might have forgotten about the meeting.
   e They ought to have let us know.
   f We needn't have reordered yet.
   g He could have walked.
   h We should have done the job ourselves.

2 a iv   b iii   c v   d i   e ii

3 LISTENING

   a The customer used the 48-hour service.
   b The parcel reference number is 672/987-POL.
   c Harriet West will call back within 15 minutes.
   d He says he delivered it, but forgot to ask for a signature.
   e Her main concern is that the parcel might have been stolen, as it was very valuable.
   f She is going to make a claim under the terms of Fast Parcel's guarantee.

D Service companies

KEY PHRASES

The company operates more than 200 contracts in the South-West.
They range in size from small to very large.
They have some big customers such as ABL and Lloyds.

We'd (We would) like you to give us a quote.
How much do you charge for this kind of work?
Could you let us know your fees?
Can I check that your commission is still 1.5%?

They are specialists in recycling.
User companies pay a fixed price for a guaranteed supply.
We hope to save more than 30% by using reconditioned pallets.

They said that they have a combined turnover of £360m.
Apparently, they employ 2000 staff.
According to their sales people, the deal is worth $300m to ABC.

They can't have said that.
They wouldn't have said that.
They must have meant $300,000.
You must have misunderstood.

They plan to extend the service to Holland soon.

INFORMATION

1 ACTIVITY

Partner B's information: You have the information below because you have recently used Sutcliffe. When **Partner A** calls you, check whether he/she has any further information. You want to know about:

- the scope of Sutcliffe's operation;
- the number of contracts they have in the region;
- their range of services;
- their existing customers;
- the company's size and status.

- Sutcliffe Catering West employ more than 2,000 staff.
- Staff undertake training in food hygiene and safety and all food handling. Staff have to pass an annual exam which tests their knowledge of food health and safety regulations.
- Sutcliffe Catering West have a design department, plan kitchen and restaurant layout, and manage the installation of equipment.

LANGUAGE NOTES

Such as, etc.

Note the following examples.

e.g. with customers such as Lloyds
in a business like this
in a case like yours
at a time such as this
in situations like this
in a company like IBM, for example
in a country such as, for example, Uganda

Fees and charges

Note the following examples.

e.g. Could you give us a quote for...?
How much do you charge for this kind of work?
You say there's no extra charge for...?
Does that figure include commission?
Our commission is 1.5%.
My fee is £2000 per day, plus expenses.
I'm afraid our rates have gone up.
We charge interest on overdue accounts.

ANSWERS

2 LANGUAGE POINTS

2 (possible answers)
law: solicitor, lawyer, judge, barrister
insurance: insurance broker, insurance salesman, claims manager
bank: bank manager, bank clerk
stock market: stock broker, dealer
dentistry: dentist, dental nurse, orthodontist
medicine: medical officer, doctor, nurse, surgeon
hotel industry: manager, receptionist, maid, barman/ barmaid, waiter/waitress
police: police officer, policeman/policewoman, inspector, constable
fire service: fire officer, fireman
information technology IT: systems analyst, business analyst, programmer
security: driver, security guard
catering: caterer, chef, cook, waiter, waitress

3 LISTENING

2 a iii b v c ii d iv e i

4 READING

1 A pallet is a platform on which goods are transported. It is usually made of wood.

2 a It supplies reconditioned pallets, and repairs those that are returned in a damaged condition.
b They can get lost, stolen or damaged.
c They hope to save more than 30% of their expenditure on pallets.
d It is worth £300,000 to Hambrook.
e They can cause serious damage to the goods being transported and make a whole load unsafe.

ENTERTAINING

A Introduction

ANSWERS

2 REVISION

2 (possible answers)
fruit: apple, pear, banana, strawberry, grapefruit
meat: chicken, beef, pork, lamb, veal
vegetables: peas, carrots, broccoli, runner beans, cauliflower
drinks: milk, fruit juice, tea, coffee, wine

3 extremely, fast, well, hard, badly

4 never, rarely, occasionally, sometimes, often, always

5 (possible answers)
a He says (that) he will get the drinks.
b She told him to go home because he wasn't well.
c They said (that) they were fully booked.

6 (possible answers)
a football
b billiards, snooker, table tennis
c football, rugby, cricket, hockey
d squash, tennis, badminton
e golf, racing
f athletics, horse-racing, greyhound-racing

B Business hospitality

KEY PHRASES

Where do you usually take your foreign clients?
Do you ever take them sightseeing?
Yes, sometimes.   No, not very often.

We occasionally take them to a club.
So do we, but very rarely.

Were you planning to do anything tomorrow night?
I was thinking of getting tickets to the opera.
I was going to invite you out to dinner.
Would you rather go to a football match?
I'd (I would) prefer to go sightseeing.

What should I wear?
Should I bring a gift?

It's (It is) an informal occasion.
You needn't (need not) wear a suit.
You don't (do not) have to bring a gift, but it's a good idea.
We mustn't (must not) be late.

Always shake hands when you are introduced.
Don't interrupt your host.
It's a good idea to carry your business cards.
It's best not to smoke.

Is there anything you don't eat?
I'm (I am) not allowed dairy products.
I can't (cannot) have anything with sugar in it.

I'm Jewish.   He's (He is) a vegetarian.
I'm on a diet.   She's (She is) diabetic.

I'm free every evening except Tuesday.

LANGUAGE NOTES

Mustn't, *needn't* and *don't have to*

We use *needn't* and *don't have to* when there is no obligation to do something.

e.g. You don't have to take a gift.
      You needn't wear a suit.

We use *mustn't* when there is an obligation not to do something.

e.g. You mustn't interrupt the host.
      I mustn't miss my train.

Would prefer and *would rather*

Note the following examples of invitations.

e.g. Would you prefer to go to a club or...?
      Would you rather go out to dinner or...?
      What would you prefer to do?
      Where would you rather go?

Note the following examples of responses.

e.g. I'd prefer to go to a night club.
      I'd rather go somewhere nearby.
      I'd prefer not to be too late.
      I'd rather not go out tonight.

ANSWERS

1 LISTENING (suggested answers)

	usually	sometimes	occasionally	very rarely
to lunch in a local restaurant	✓			
to dinner in central London		✓		
sightseeing			✓	
to the theatre			✓	
to a football match			✓	
to a cricket match				✓

3 LANGUAGE POINTS

1 **a** mustn't
   b needn't / don't have to
   c needn't / don't have to
   d needn't / don't have to
   e mustn't
   f mustn't / needn't / don't have to
   g mustn't
   h needn't / don't have to

C Hotels and restaurants

KEY PHRASES

Shall we have a drink in the bar before we eat?
Let's (Let us) leave our coats with the porter.

Do you have a reservation?
I booked a table for eight o'clock.
Mary, would you (like to) sit there?

Excuse me, we're (we are) ready to order.
I'd (I would) like the beef.
I'll (I will) have the prawn salad.
And to follow?
Can I have it as a main course?
How do you like your steak?
Medium rare.

So what does the article say?
It says that generally, if you invite someone to a meal, you should pay the bill.

Did you speak to John?
Did you talk to him about it?

He said that they had excellent conference facilities.
They told me to book a room with a view of the sea.
We asked the receptionist to prepare the bill.

Let's begin.   How's (How is) your food?
Let's drink to success.   Cheers!

Could you put the drinks on my bill, please?
How much do you usually tip?
Service is included.

LANGUAGE NOTES

Toasts and tipping

Note these phrases for making a toast.

e.g. Here's to you.
    Here's to the new project.
    Let's drink to success.

Your very good health!
Cheers!
I'd like to propose a toast to...

Note these phrases for leaving a tip.

e.g. Should I leave a tip?
    Do you usually leave a tip?
    How much should I tip them?
    Is service included?
    Is 10% enough (as a tip)?

Some examples of reported speech

Reporting statements:
He said (that) they had excellent facilities.
She told me (that) she would make the bookings.
He said (that) he would call me the following day.
He mentioned (that) he had stayed there the year before.

Reporting questions:
I asked him where the restaurant was.
He asked me if I could recommend a starter.
They wanted to know if they should leave a tip.
They asked me whether we had any vacancies in the following week.

Making requests and giving advice:
We asked the receptionist to bring the bill.
They told me not to drink the water.
I advised him (not) to have the soup.
He told me to book a room with a view of the sea.

Say, tell, speak and talk

Note the following examples of *say*.

e.g. What did he say to you?
    He always says the same thing.
    She said (that) she'd be late.

Note the following examples of *tell*.

e.g. What did he tell you?

He always tells them what he thinks.
Could you tell me the time, please?
They told us not to wait.

Note the following examples of *speak*.

e.g. We need to speak to our lawyer about this.
I'd like to speak to John, please.
Do you speak Arabic?
Please speak more slowly – I can't understand.

Note the following examples of *talk*.

e.g. We need to talk to our lawyer about this.
Who was that woman you were talking to?
He talks too much.

ANSWERS

1 LISTENING

	Starter	Main course
Ralph	onion soup	steak
Mary	–	prawn salad
Hiroshi	salmon	chicken peri peri

2 ACTIVITY (possible answer)

g, n, i, l, d, j, b, m, f, a, h, c, e, k

3 LANGUAGE POINTS (suggested answers)

2 a He said (that) they have/had excellent conference facilities.
  b He told me to ask for a room with a sea view.
  c She said (that) she would have the beef.
  d He advised me not to order the fish because it wasn't very good there.

e They said (that) they had been out for lunch the previous day.
OR: They said (that) they went out...
f Ralph said (that) they were all going out for dinner the following night.
g He asked how much they usually tipped.

3 a told   e speak
  b said   f talk
  c speak/talk g say
  d talk/speak h speak/talk

INFORMATION

4 READING

Partner B's information:

As a general rule, the person who invites someone else to a business meal should pay. There are exceptions to this rule, however.

Example: You invite another manager to a casual lunch for strictly social reasons. He brings his wife along. In this case, the other manager should offer to pay the bill, since he brought a guest.

Example: Two managers agree to have lunch together. Even though one advanced the idea, it is agreed in advance that they will split the bill.

From *The Little Black Book of Business Etiquette*, by Michael C.Thomsett

D Corporate entertaining

KEY PHRASES

The event will include at least 100 aircraft.
It begins at 10 am and lasts four hours.

We're (We are) located in the main hospitality complex.
We are conveniently close to all the attractions.
Our premises offer a superb view of the proceedings.

The package we provide includes a four-course lunch.
  full bar facilities
  souvenir programmes

Our experienced team will ensure...
  ...that your day runs smoothly.
  ...that everything goes well.

Can I make a booking?
I'd (I would) like the standard package.
Can I make a couple of changes?

Have you thought of having music?
Why don't you have a cold buffet instead?
That's (That is) a good idea.
I'm (I am) not sure about that.

I'll (I will) confirm this next week.
I really need to know sooner than that.
Could you get back to me earlier than that?
We can do it more quickly, if you like.

It's (It is) a very close race.
They're (They are) playing well.
Good shot!

117

INFORMATION

4 ACTIVITY

Partner B's information: You have a party of 20 to entertain. You would like to know:

a what is special about the event;
b how much it costs per person;
c what date the event takes place;
d what time it begins;
e how long it lasts.

Think about what you require:

- a cordoned-off area?
- use of telephones?
- toilets?
- easily accessible free parking?
- coffee, lunch and tea?
- bar facilities?

LANGUAGE NOTES

Adverbs

Most adjectives:
quick – quickly
careful – carefully

Adjectives ending in -le:
possible – possibly
profitable – profitably

Adjectives ending in -ic:
automatic – automatically
realistic – realistically

Adjectives ending in -y:
easy – easily
temporary – temporarily

Common exceptions:
hard – hard
early – early
public – publicly
long – long
little – little

Examples:
We ensure that everything runs smoothly.
I completely disagree.
She hardly ever takes time off work.
Everything went extremely well.
Their prices are fairly high.
He earns very little.
Realistically, you shouldn't expect an answer until tomorrow.

Comparative adverbs

Short adverbs:
hard – harder
soon – sooner
early – earlier

Longer adverbs:
frequently – more frequently
efficient – more efficiently

Common exceptions:
well – better
badly – worse
little – less

Examples:
He has been working here longer than me.
It runs more smoothly now.
We need a decision faster than that.
The sooner, the better.

Making suggestions

Note the following examples.

e.g. Can I make a suggestion?
I would recommend taking them to a sports event.
I think you should book it now.
You could move it to the following day.
Have you thought of having live music?
Why not have a buffet instead?
How about booking the tickets tomorrow?
If I were you, I'd discuss it with Keith.

ANSWERS

1 READING (possible answers)

  a Someone will meet them on arrival and escort them to the club.
  b It lasts eight hours.
  c Yes, there is.
  d It stands for 'very important person'.

2 LISTENING (possible answer)

The client doesn't want floral arrangements or accompanying music. Instead of a four-course lunch, she would like a cold buffet. She only wants the use of one phone and one fax machine, and she requests that all drinks are put on their bill.

3 LANGUAGE POINTS (suggested answers)

  1 a I totally agree with you.
    b The reception went extremely well.
    c I read the information quickly.
    d We rarely take visitors to the theatre.
    e I drove to work slowly this morning.
    f Driving conditions were terribly difficult.
    g She organised everything brilliantly.
    h Surprisingly, she didn't forget anything.

2 a more smoothly   e better
  b earlier   f more often
  c harder   g worse
  d more slowly   h sooner

3 a snooker, golf, badminton, table tennis, squash, football, rugby
  b snooker, golf, badminton, table tennis, squash, rugby
  c boxing, wrestling

  d snooker, golf, badminton, table tennis, squash, football, rugby
  e boxing, wrestling, golf, badminton, table tennis, squash, football, rugby
  f swimming, sailing, motor racing
  g football, rugby
  h boxing, wrestling, golf
  i football, rugby

UNIT 7

MEETINGS

A Introduction

ANSWERS

1 a So do I. / I do too. (I think so too.)
  b Neither do I. / I don't either. (I don't think so either.)
  c So do I. / I do too. (I believe so too.)
  d Neither do I. / I don't either. (I don't believe so either.)

2 (possible answers)
  a What will you do if they cancel the meeting?
  b If the weather is good, I will go for a walk.
  c If they don't come, we will have more time available.
  d I won't buy it if it isn't completely reliable.

3 a on
  b before, after
  c about
  d at

4 a She asked Mary to take the minutes.
  b She told Mary to take the minutes.
  c She wanted Mary to take the minutes.
  d She said that Mary could/should take the minutes.
    (OR: She said that she would like Mary to take the minutes.)

5 a 2   b 3   c 1   d 4

B Setting up a meeting

KEY PHRASES

The meeting is on Friday the 23rd.
We're (We are) meeting at ten o'clock.
It's (It is) taking place at Queens House.
We're holding the meeting in room 406.

We need to discuss the sales report.
We're meeting to talk about the new contract.
I'll (I will) send you a copy of the agenda.

Are you still OK for the 27th?
Can you make the meeting?
Could you let me know by the weekend at the latest?

I'm (I am) having some problems at this end.
It looks as if Friday is going to be difficult.
It looks as though the room isn't (is not) available.

I thought I'd (I had) better call you.
We'd (We had) better postpone the meeting.
We'd better meet at the airport instead.

Would you be able to meet on Saturday?
Is she going to be able to make the meeting?
I suggest that we all meet up for lunch on Saturday.

The meeting has been put off till Thursday.
It's (It has) been delayed till 3.15.
It's been moved to the boardroom.

If I don't (do not) hear from you, I'll (I will) assume that everything is OK.

LANGUAGE NOTES

Had better

Note the following examples.

e.g. I'd (I had) better check with my boss.
We'd (We had) better postpone the meeting.
You'd (You had) better not mention that.
Had he better call to confirm? No, it's not necessary.
Had we better meet at the airport instead? Yes, we'd better.

Some uses of *to be able to*

Note how we use *be able to* instead of *can* and *could*.

e.g. I wasn't able to get there in time.
(I couldn't get there in time.)
She isn't able to attend the meeting.
(She can't attend the meeting)

Note how we use the infinitive form.

e.g. He'd like to be able to attend the conference.
We should be able to make a decision then.

Note how we use the *-ing* form.

e.g. I enjoy being able to walk to work.
It's hard to get a job here without being able to drive.

Punctuation

Some common terms:

. full stop   - dash
, comma   " " inverted commas
: colon   ? question mark
; semi colon   ! exclamation mark

Some useful phrases:
The heading should be underlined.
That phrase should be in italics/capitals.
That word begins with a capital letter.
That sentence should be in inverted commas.
Leave a line.
Begin at the margin.
New paragraph.   Next line.

Rearranging a meeting

Note the following phrases.

e.g. Could we postpone the meeting until Friday?
Could we put it off till the end of the week?
We could move it to next week.
Is it possible to change the date?
It has been moved to the boardroom.
It has been delayed till 3.15.
We'll have to cancel the meeting.
We'll have to call it off.

ANSWERS

1 READING

a 22nd May, 11 am; to Phillip, from John
b 21st May, 10 am; to Phillip, from John
c 21st May, 3.30 pm; to John, from Phillip

2 LISTENING

The order is: c, d, f, a, e, b

3 LANGUAGE POINTS

1 a can't
   b be able to
   c be able to
   d be able to
   e can/could
   f being able to
   g couldn't
   h be able to

2 a You look/sound as if/though you don't agree.
   b It looks/sounds as if/though we'd better postpone the meeting.
   c It looks/sounds as if/though the room isn't available.
   d You look/sound as if/though you need a holiday.
   e Your car looks/sounds as if/though it needs repairing.
   f He sounds as if/though he is Spanish.

C Procedure

KEY PHRASES

Shall we begin?
There's (There is) a lot to get through.

Has everyone got an agenda?
There are four main topics on the agenda.
Let's (Let us) start with item one.

Our main aim is to approve the budget increases.
Mark, what's (what is) your opinion?
I believe you wanted to say something about this.

As you know, I'm (I am) in favour of the plan.
I have to say, I'm opposed to spending any more.
I agree with that.
I'm afraid I disagree completely.
I agree up to a point.

Let's recap.
Can we deal with that point later?
Can we move on to the next item?

In the first paragraph, it says smoking will be banned.
In the next line, it refers to 'communal areas'.

If they didn't (did not) smoke, most smokers would support the policy.
If I were you, I'd (I would) check the facts.

Shall we vote on the proposal?
Those in favour? Those against?
I suggest we leave it there.

LANGUAGE NOTES

The Second Conditional

Affirmative:
I would come to the meeting if I had time.
If we knew her number, we could call her.
If I were you, I'd check the figures.

Negative:
If I didn't like the job, I wouldn't stay.
If he couldn't drive, he would have to learn.
Most smokers would support the policy if they didn't smoke.

Interrogative:
Would it be more convenient if we started earlier?
Would they mind if we postponed the meeting?
What would happen if somebody was ill?

Short answers:

Yes, it would.	No, it wouldn't.
Yes, they would.	No, they wouldn't.

Referring to documents

Note the following phrases.

e.g. In the third paragraph, line five, it says...
In the fourth sentence down, it states...
In the next line, it refers to...
If you look at page four, there is a reference to...
...at the top/bottom of the second column...
...at the beginning/end of paragraph two...
...in the middle of column/paragraph one...
...just above/below that...

ANSWERS

1 LISTENING (possible answers)

1 a No, they hadn't.
   The traffic was terrible.
 b Bill is going to take the minutes.
   Its purpose is to approve increases in the building budget.
 c They are talking about whether to spend more money on the building programme.
   No, he doesn't.
 d Yes, it is.
   She abstains.

2 The following phrases from the list on page 137 are used in the dialogues:

 a Shall we begin?

We only have one hour.
 b Has everyone got an agenda?
   Let's start with item one.
   I believe you wanted to say something about...
   As you know...
 c Mark, what's your opinion...?
   I have to say that I'm opposed to...
   I agree with that.
 d Shall we vote on the proposal then?
   Those in favour?
   Those against?
   Are you abstaining?
   I suggest we leave it there.

2 LANGUAGE POINTS

1 a If we paid them enough, they wouldn't go on strike.
 b If we paid off our bank loans, we wouldn't have the bank on our backs.
 c If I was/were in charge, I would ban smoking at work.
 d If we had ISO accreditation, our customers wouldn't stop buying from us.
 e If we didn't have so many meetings, we would get some work done.
 f If we didn't spend so much on entertaining clients, there would be money for training.
 g If they didn't smoke, they would support the ban.
 h If I were you, I would give up smoking.
   OR: If I were in your position, I would give up smoking.

2 (possible answers)

	Agreement	Disagreement
Absolutely.	✓	
Come off it!		✓
Rubbish!		✓
I'm not sure I agree with that.		✓
Definitely.	✓	
I don't know.	–	–
I don't agree with that.		✓
That's right.	✓	
I'm afraid I disagree completely.		✓
I agree with you up to a point.	✓	
I agree with most of what you say.	✓	
Yes, but...	✓	
Not necessarily.		✓

3 READING AND LISTENING

2 Production considerations   [ ]
  Special areas for smokers   [✓]
  Company policy on smoking   [✓]
  Counselling for smokers   [ ]
  Resistance of smokers   [✓]
  Penalties   [ ]
  Reaction of hourly-paid workers   [✓]
  Positive action (anti-smoking posters, etc.)   [✓]

D Follow-up

KEY PHRASES

How did the meeting go?
Did you manage to get through the agenda?
Did the meeting overrun?

It went very well. We covered a lot of ground.
We didn't (did not) manage to cover all the points, but we agreed to meet again next week.

Who chaired it?
Did anyone take minutes?
Are they going to circulate the minutes?

Anita proposed that Owen should chair the meeting.
Pilar suggested that they should raise the matter then.

What's (What is) the position with NAK?
Were you able to contact the contractor?
How are you getting on with point five?

I thought you were going to send me your proposals.
Did you remember to send a copy to the MD?

To be honest, I'm (I am) not sure I did.
Frankly, I've (I have) been so busy, I simply haven't (have not) had time.
I'm planning to do it tomorrow.

He managed to send the proposal, as agreed.
We've (We have) sent you the action points, as promised.
It's (It is) all taken care of.

When is the next meeting?
We arranged to meet again on the 11th.

INFORMATION

3 LANGUAGE POINTS

3 **Partner B:** Ask **Partner A** about a meeting he/she has attended recently. The following questions may help you.

> **Useful language**
>
> How did the meeting go?
> Did you manage to cover everything?
> Did you manage to get through the agenda?
> Did you start on time?
> Did you run out of time?
> Did the meeting overrun?
> Who chaired it?
> Did anyone take minutes?
> Are they going to circulate the minutes?
> When is the next meeting?

LANGUAGE NOTES

More reported speech

Note the following examples.

e.g. 'Will it be ready on time?'
  She asked if it would be ready on time.
  She wondered if it would be ready on time.
  She wanted to know if it would be ready on time.

  'I think we should hire a bigger room.'
  He said that we should hire a bigger room.
  He thought that we should hire a bigger room.
  He proposed that we should hire a bigger room.
  He suggested that we should hire a bigger room.

  'Could you report back at the next meeting?'
  He asked her to report back at the next meeting.
  He told her to report back at the next meeting.
  He wants her to report back at the next meeting.

ANSWERS

1 READING

1 Fabio Mercotzi is probably equal in position to Pilar Hernandez.

2

```
* PH to contact NAK Supplies:
  - re. changes in delivery
  procedures; ✓
  - to enquire about price
  reductions.
* PH to arrange meeting with NAK's
  MD to discuss credit limits. ✓
* FM to send a more detailed outline
  of proposal to NAK and HG. ✓
* HG to check how the changes affect
  the insurance position.
* FM to send PH notes on handling
  the money question.
```

2 LISTENING

a He can't remember. He probably has, but has lost it.
b She was expecting to receive some new ideas on how to handle the money question.
c He hasn't had time to.
d Fabio and Pilar disagree about this. Fabio thinks they are, but Pilar is not so sure.
e He can't check the insurance if he doesn't have the details.
f She promises to call back later that afternoon.

3 LANGUAGE POINTS

1 (possible answers)
a Anita said (that) she thought Owen should chair the meeting.
She proposed that Owen should chair the meeting.
b Ivan asked who was going to take the minutes.
He wanted to know who was going to take the minutes.

c Lupe wondered why we/they didn't demand compensation.
She suggested that we/they should demand compensation.
d Franz thought (that) we/they should cancel the order.
He proposed that we/they should cancel the order.

UNIT 8

TRAVEL

A Introduction

ANSWERS

3 (possible answers)
I would like to reserve a single room, please.
Can I get you a cup of coffee?
Hello, is that room service?
The souvenir shop is on the ground floor by the main entrance.
Excuse me, I'd like to change rooms – this one is very noisy.
Do you have a vacancy on the 16th of next month?
I'm planning to stay in Dallas for two nights.

4 a by rail
b by car/bus/taxi
c by air
d by sea

6 a a sudden decision
b a prediction
c a promise

B Arranging a visit

KEY PHRASES

I'm (I am) calling on behalf of Ms Braun.
She'll (She will) be visiting the States in July.
She'll be staying in Boston for six days.
She'd (She would) like to see you while she's (she is) there.
She would like to visit you during her stay.

When does your flight arrive?
When do you get to Kuala Lumpur?
How long will you be staying in Singapore?

What's (What is) her flight number?
What's your departure time?
What's their ETA?

Will you be coming by taxi?
Yes, we will.   No, we won't (will not).

Tell the cab driver to take the Sumner Tunnel.
Then get on the Expressway South.

Take the turnpike to the first exit.
Follow the signs to Allston.
Turn left at the fourth set of lights.

This time next week, she'll be in the States.
In two years' time, I'll still be working in the bank.

We look forward to meeting you.
I hope to meet you while you're (you are) here.

LANGUAGE NOTES

The Future Continuous tense

Affirmative:
They will be waiting for you...
I will be looking for a new job...

Negative:
I'm afraid we won't be coming.
She won't be expecting your call.

Interrogative:
Will you be meeting each other in Vancouver?
Will they be travelling to Ipoh by car?

Short answers:

Yes, we will.   No, we won't.
Yes, they will.   No, they won't.

Examples:
We won't be visiting the States in July.
Will he be coming by taxi?
This time next week, she will be in Boston.
In two years' time, I'll still be working for a bank.

INFORMATION

4 ACTIVITY

Partner **B**'s information: Call **Partner A** for the
information you need to finalise his/her itinerary.

ITINERARY	
23rd Nov	Arrival at Kuala Lumpur airport, on flight number _____, arriving at 2.30 pm.
24th Nov	Visit to _____.
25th Nov	_____ to Ipoh.
26th Nov	Meeting with _____.
27th Nov	Return to Kuala Lumpur airport. Singapore Airlines, flight SL 739 to _____ leaving at _____.

Useful language	
When	will you be arriving in...?
	does your flight get into...?
How	are you getting to...?
Who	do you visit/meet in...?
What	is [your departure time]?
	is [your ETA]?

ANSWERS

1 READING

1 Her company wants to set up a relationship with an American partner.

2
a	on	f	with
b	on	g	in
c	with	h	to
d	in	i	for
e	to	j	at

2 LISTENING

1 Tell the cab driver to take the Sumner Tunnel...
2 Take the Mass Pike west to the first exit...
3 Leave Mass Pike here...
4 Go to the fourth set of lights, and turn left...
5 Go down Harvard, and take your first left again...
6 We are the fifth house on the right...

3 LANGUAGE POINTS (possible answers)

3 a Are you travelling
   b I'll see
   c are you doing
   d I'm meeting
   e will they be leaving
   f they'll be arriving
   g I'll see you
   h will be going

5
a	while	e	during
b	during	f	for
c	while	g	while
d	for	h	during

C Abroad on business

KEY PHRASES

I find it difficult to sleep on long-haul flights.
Do you? I don't (do not). I just take a sleeping pill.

It's (It is) easy to cope with jet lag.
Do you think so? I find it quite difficult.

I'll (I will) take a pill as soon as I'm (I am) on the plane.
I won't (will not) have another meal till I get to Berlin.
Will you see John before he leaves?
Where will you be staying while you're (you are) here?

It's four star rather than five star.
I usually go by train rather than fly.
We're (We are) meeting in Paris rather than Lille.

Can I have a return ticket to Paris, please?
Have you got a single room for Thursday?
Is there a toilet we can use?

Are there any delays?
There are some roadworks up the road.
There have been terrible jams.
Thanks for the warning.

Do your rates include insurance?
They include everything except petrol.

So how much do I owe you?
£35 altogether.
Can you sent the bill to Rembola Ltd for the attention of Anna Sogat?
Sure. Could you sign here, please?

LANGUAGE NOTES

Easy/Difficult to, etc.

Note these examples of adjectives followed by *to*.

e.g. The directions are easy to follow.
      I find it difficult to drive on the left.
      It's important to decide now.
      It's not necessary to book a seat.
      It's quite common to have delays.
      It's quicker and cheaper to go by car.

When, as soon as, while, before, etc.

Note how we use *when, as soon as, while, before,* etc. in future sentences.

e.g. Will you see John before he leaves?
      Where will you be staying while you are here?
      I won't sleep until I get to Berlin.
      As soon as we hear from them, we'll let you know.
      After you pass the station, you'll see a factory on your right.
      I'll call you as we're leaving.

ANSWERS

2 LANGUAGE POINTS

2 a When I see her, I'll give her your regards.
  b I won't sleep until I get to New York.
  c Will you be able to do it before you go?
  d As soon as I get to my hotel, I'll have a bath.
  e Will you be working while you're in France?
  f I'll let you know when they call the flight.
  g I'll call you as soon as the taxi is here.

  h Where will you be staying while you're in Berlin?

3 **air:** jet-lag, customs, travel sickness, overbooking, transfer desk, long-haul flight, duty free, runway, landing
   sea: customs, travel sickness, overbooking, hydrofoil, ferry terminal, duty free, landing
   land: customs, travel sickness, overbooking, dual carriageway, toll bridge, filling station, parking meter, buffet car, chauffeur, level crossing

3 LISTENING AND ACTIVITY

1 (possible answers)
a No, they only have rooms with showers.
b It includes a full English or American breakfast.
c He wants the bill to be sent to Rembola Ltd, marked for the attention of Anna Sogat.
d The passenger is travelling on the 16.56 train.
e It is a good idea because that train is normally very busy.
f He wants to pay by Visa.
g The customer needs to pay for petrol and oil.
h He recommends the B road because there are roadworks ahead which have caused terrible traffic jams all week.
i He has to leave the main road at the next exit.
j The customer is looking for a four-door saloon.
k The company's rates include everything except petrol, oil and accident waiver.
l He wants it immediately.

2 (possible answers)
a hotel, restaurant, theatre, etc.
b railway station, bus station
c airport check-in
d airport, hotel, etc.
e office, street, taxi, friend or colleague's car
f bank
g shop, market
h hotel reception
i taxi, friend or colleague's car
j shop, office, hotel, friend or colleague's house, etc.
k car hire firm
l office, filling station, shop, bar, etc.

D Reporting back

KEY PHRASES

I'm (I am) just back from a trip to Brazil.
I made some good contacts while I was there.

It's (It is) the largest country in Latin America.
It's divided into nine economic areas.
It's among the 20 richest countries worldwide.

It's a member of LAFTA.
What does LAFTA stand for?

Minas Gerais is the third most important state in the region.
   second largest   fourth richest
São Paulo accounts for 55% of the country's output.
It has a population of 33 million.
The main industries are mining and steel production.

How far is it to São Paulo?
Not far.   A long way.
It's further than you think.

How long does it take to get there?
Not long.   A long time.
Does it take long by plane?

What were you doing there?
How long were you there?
What was your hotel like?
Where is Nevtchugansk exactly?
It's north-east of Chelyabinsk.

I'll (I will) write my report today, in case they need it tomorrow.
If I finish it before you go home, I'll let you have a copy.

INFORMATION

1 READING

Partner B: You wrote the report on page 74. When **Partner A** calls with further questions, reply using the information below.

- Mercosul is the common market of the area. The members are Brazil, Paraguay, Uruguay and Argentina.
- The population of São Paulo is 33 million.
- If São Paulo were an independent country, it would be among the 20 richest worldwide.
- Rio de Janeiro is the same size as Denmark.
- Shipbuilding is a major industry in Rio.
- Minas Gerais has a population of 12 million.
- In Minas Gerais, there are opportunities for export in the textile industry.
- Rio Grande do Sul is one of Brazil's biggest agricultural areas.

LANGUAGE NOTES

Some acronyms

ASEAN = Association of South East Asian Nations
EC   = European Community
G7   = Group of Seven (leading industrial nations)
GATT = General Agreement on Tariffs and Trade
GDP   = Gross Domestic Product
IMF   = International Monetary Fund
NAFTA = North American Free Trade Area
NATO = North Atlantic Treaty Organisation
OPEC = Organisation of Petroleum-Exporting Countries
UN   = United Nations
WHO   = World Health Organisation

Rankings

Note the following examples.

e.g. the third most important state in the region
the second largest company in the world
the fourth richest country in Latin America
the second most expensive city in Europe

In case

Note the following examples.

e.g. I faxed the report in case he needed it today.
Ring me on Monday in case I have some news.
We'd better call them in case they're waiting.
I'll take a spare one in case we run out.

ANSWERS

2 LISTENING

2 The speaker likes Nevtchugansk and is looking forward to going back.

a F   b T   c T   d T   e F   f T

3 LANGUAGE POINTS

2 a in case   e If
   b If   f in case
   c in case   g in case
   d If   h if

MONEY AND FINANCE

A Introduction

ANSWERS

1 a earn
   b spend
   c costs
   d charges
   e pay

2 a ¾ (three quarters)
   b ¼ (a quarter)
   c ½ (a half)
   d ⅓ (a third)

3 a The company was founded in 1962.
      When was the company founded?
   b We are paid by cheque.
      How are you paid?

c Our brochures are printed in Korea.
   Where are your brochures printed?
d The work will be finished by three o'clock.
   When will the work be finished?

4 (possible answers)
   We spend a lot on raw materials.
   I buy very few magazines.
   I don't spend much on entertaining.
   We don't buy very much aluminium.

5 (possible answers)
   account number, bank balance, bank statement,
   cheque book, cheque card, credit card,
   cash dispenser, exchange rate, interest rate,
   travellers' cheque

B Personal finances

KEY PHRASES

Our food bill is quite big.
We spend a lot of money on groceries.
We spend very little on holidays.
We did go abroad for a week last year, but that was
exceptional.

I do spend money on hobbies, but not very much.
I'm (I am) very keen on sailing.
That's an expensive pastime.

About 24% of my income goes in tax.
We pay our regular outgoings by direct debit.
I can't (cannot) afford to run two cars.
I need to clear my overdraft.

Your commitments are the same as mine.
Her situation is very different from his.
It's (It is) not so different – they both have children.

How much did she spend on entertainment?
What's (What is) the figure for depreciation?
Her expenditure on secretarial expenses is up.
Expenditure on postage is similar to last year.

We normally spend about half as much as that.
   twice as much as she does
   far more than that on insurance

Our home was broken into.
They took my video.
It's worth about £300.
Are you insured?
Yes, I'll (I will) have to make a claim.

LANGUAGE NOTES

Do and did for emphasis

We use do/did for emphasis and to correct
misunderstandings. Note the following examples.

e.g. He does have the account number.
      We did send you the tax form.
      I did enjoy your talk.
      We do spend money on hobbies, but not much.
      We did go away for a week last year, but that was
      exceptional.

Some insurance terms

Note the following examples.

e.g. Are you insured?
      The premium was paid on the first of January.
      Are you covered for theft?
      Can you arrange cover for...?
      We need to renew our policy.
      We'll have to make a claim.
      Could you send me a claim form?

Fractions and multiples

Fractions:
She earns half as much as he does.
She earns half of what he does.
We normally spend a quarter of that.

Multiples:
They spend twice as much on housing as we do.
Their taxes are double ours.
Their advertising budget is three times the size of ours.

ANSWERS

1 LISTENING

charities	[ ]
eating out	[✓]
clothes	[ ]
foreign travel	[ ]
religious activities	[ ]
DIY	[✓]
food and groceries	[✓]
theatre and other arts events	[ ]
stocks and shares	[ ]
children	[✓]
cars	[ ]
books	[ ]
antiques	[✓]
sport: sailing, golf, etc.	[✓]

2 LANGUAGE POINTS

1 a goes   e clear
   b keep   f spend
   c pay   g afford
   d earns   h cash

3 READING (possible answers)

They learned that if you make a false claim, you may be found out.

a Their home was broken into and their television and video were stolen.
b They thought they would do it by adding a few items to their insurance claim.
c He was caught by the police.
d They were prosecuted and fined £200 each.

INFORMATION

4 ACTIVITY

Partner B's information:

SALLY VOIGHT PRODUCTIONS LTD
PROFIT & LOSS ACCOUNT FOR THE YEAR ENDED 31 AUGUST

	Current year	Last year
Turnover (fee income)	163,141	159,244
ADMINISTRATIVE EXPENSES		
Secretarial assistant	15,000	–
Wardrobe / clothing	3,666	4,477
Travelling, accommodation & subsistence	8,791	....
Lighting & heating	....	2,281
Motor expenses	2,612	2,163
Telephone & postage	....	3,446
Professional books, journals & subscriptions	1,350	1,229
....	2,566	2,620
Photography	–	....
Company registration expenses	25	40
Company pension plan	36,167	32,692
Director's remuneration & NIC	80,604	97,198
Depreciation	300	300
Audit and accountancy	3,100	2,200
Sundry expenses	316	994
....	989	989
Cleaning	920	760
Theatre visits & research expenses	....	105
	159.174	165.365
Operating profit / (loss)	3,967	(6,232)
Interest receivable & similar income	842	757
....	(106)	(377)
Other operating income	–	–
Profit / (loss) on ordinary activities before taxation	4,703	(5,741)
Taxation on ordinary activities	–	–
Profit / (loss) on ordinary activities after taxation	4,703	(5,741)
Balance brought forward	10,561	....
Balance carried forward	15,264	£10,561

Useful language

How much did she spend on [lighting and heating]?
What's the figure for [theatre visits]?
What's the figure of [£2,566] for?
What does the figure of [£989] represent?

C Company finances

KEY PHRASES

In November, the company announced its results.
The balance sheet presents a favourable picture.

What's (What is) the value of your fixed assets?
What are your current liabilities?
How much do you owe?
What's the total value of the company?

Net assets are in the region of £40m.
Gross liabilities are just over £10m.
The company is valued at between 20 and 30 million dollars.

A key factor in these results is the quality of our management team.
Our aim is to meet our customers' needs profitably.

What was your turnover in the period?
What were your total sales?
How much profit did you make?
What was the dividend last year?

Productivity increased by 6.5%.
The quality of our service improved.
Overall revenue increased by 5.7% over the period.
Domestic sales accounted for 33% of our total revenue.

This was achieved by offering value for money.
    better service   greater choice
Tough targets have been set for the coming year.

The accounts were approved at the AGM.

LANGUAGE NOTES

Some forms of the Passive

(See page 109 for notes on the Present Simple Passive tense.)

Affirmative:
The meeting has been postponed.
The accounts were approved at the AGM.
The result will be announced next week.
The new factory is going to be built in China.

Negative:
The accounts haven't been audited yet.
The agent's commission wasn't included.
This package shouldn't be sent by ordinary post.
The report isn't going to be completed before Friday.

Interrogative:
What has been decided?
Were the recommendations accepted?
Could it be sent by registered mail?
How is the project going to be financed?

Some business abbreviations

APR = Annual Percentage Rate

attn = for the attention of
cc = copies to
co = company
dept = department
ECU = European Currency Unit
encl = enclosed
ext = extension (number)
HQ = headquarters
PA = personal assistant
PIN = personal identity number
PLC = public limited company
PR = public relations
re. = regarding, in connection with
ref. = reference
VIP = very important person

ANSWERS

1 READING

a fixed assets
b creditors
c shareholders
d current assets/stock
e loans
f revaluation reserve
g current assets/debtors
h deferred taxation
i past profits

2 LANGUAGE POINTS

1 (possible answers)
a Have targets been set for the coming year?
(Yes, they were set in March.)
b When will the new prices be announced?
(They'll be announced next week.)
c Were the accounts approved at the AGM?
(Yes, they were.)
d How can management performance be measured?
(It can be measured by various different indicators.)
e How much is owed by the company?
(Five million pounds is owed by the company.)
f Have the funds been transferred yet?
(Yes, they were transferred today.)
g Where is the new plant going to be located?
(It is probably going to be located in Taiwan.)

2 (possible answer)
'The company is currently valued at about $20 million. Last year, tough financial targets were set, which were met without difficulty. In the accounting period to the end of December, profits were increased by more than 15%. These results were announced in January, and the accounts were approved by the AGM in March. Equivalent targets have been established for the current year.'

3 a value added tax
   b account
   c annual general meeting
   d bring/brought forward
   e I owe you
   f please turn over
   g retail price index
   h personal computer
   i balance
   j outstanding, out of stock/service, on sale
   k pay as you earn
   l information technology

3 LISTENING

1 In November, the Civil Aviation Authority announced its new pricing formula.

2 The new pricing formula sets tough targets for the coming period.

3 In the year to the end of March 1992, productivity increased by 6.5%.

4 Staff members were reduced and the quality of the service improved.

5 BAA increased overall revenue by expanding airport retailing.

6 Retailing revenue per passenger increased by 5.7% over 1990/91.

7 Retail expansion will continue with the opening of 90 new shops.

8 A key factor in these results is the quality of BAA's management team.

D Payment

KEY PHRASES

I'm (I am) calling in connection with our invoice of May 27th.
Can we pay you by cheque?
We'd (We would) prefer to be paid in cash.

We don't (do not) appear to have received payment.
The invoice is still outstanding.
It was due for payment on the 26th.

I'm sorry, but we have no record of your invoice.
Could you give me the details?
What was the invoice number?
   the invoice value   the payment date

It was for 25 training manuals at £25 each.
The invoice value was 5000 Swedish krona plus 22½% VAT.

It seems that it was passed for payment on the 10th.
According to our records, it was paid two weeks ago.

We haven't (have not) settled your bill for the simple reason that we haven't received the goods.
Apparently, there was a query on this.
That's (That is) why we haven't paid it yet.
Didn't you receive our letter?

When can we expect payment?
Leave it with me.
I'll (I will) arrange for a cheque to be sent immediately.

We'll (We will) take no further action providing we receive payment within 14 days.
I'll assume everything is OK unless I hear from you.

LANGUAGE NOTES

Apparently, it seems that, etc.

Note the following examples.

e.g. Apparently, there was a query on this.
      We don't appear to have received it.
      You seem to have paid twice.
      It appears that they sent the payment last week.
      It seems that it was passed for payment on the 10th.

Unless and *providing/provided*

Note the following examples.

e.g. We will take no further action provided we receive payment within 14 days.
      Providing you fax it today, it'll be in time.
      He's arriving at 8.30 unless there's a delay.
      Unless I hear from you, I'll assume everything is OK.

Each and *every*

Note the following examples relating to invoices and payment.

e.g. They cost £50 each.
      Each copy costs £25.
      Every invoice is checked before it leaves my office.
      We have a computer run every Friday.

ANSWERS

1 READING

The letter is probably a first reminder.

2 LANGUAGE POINTS

2 a provided/providing
   b provided/providing
   c unless
   d provided/providing

e unless
f unless
g provided/providing
h unless

3 a by   e on
   b in   f against
   c on/for   g by
   d at   h in

4 a Let's split the cost fifty fifty.
   b It'll cost between three hundred and five hundred dollars.
   c What is five thousand divided by three hundred and twenty-five?
   d What is five point three (multiplied) by eight point seven?
      OR: What is five point three times eight point seven?
   e Five thousand five hundred (five and a half thousand) Swedish krona plus twenty-two and a half per cent VAT
   f What is five point nought nought four minus/less four point three four six?
   g The tank has a capacity of sixty cubic metres.
   h The plant covers an area of five hundred square metres.
   i Two fifths of our production is exported.
   j Bad debts are about three and a half per cent of debts outstanding.
      OR: Bad debts roughly equal three and a half per cent of outstanding debts.

3 ACCENTS AND PRONUNCIATION

a iii   b ii   c iv   d v   e i

4 LISTENING AND ACTIVITY

INFORMATION

1 READING

Sample letter:

Dear Ms Ashok,

YOUR INVOICE NO. 3947 of 29TH JANUARY
FOR £2,175.00

I am writing with reference to your
letter of _____, relating to the
above invoice. According to our
records, this was paid by bank transfer
on _____.

The details are as follows:
Our bank reference: _____
Your bank reference: _____
Transfer number: _____
Date: _____

We would be grateful if you could
confirm that the payment has now
reached you.

Yours sincerely,

4 LISTENING AND ACTIVITY

Partner B's information:

Useful language
It was due for payment on _____
Payment is now outstanding/overdue.
The delivery note was signed by _____.
We haven't received anything.
What was the date of your letter/payment?
When can we expect settlement?
Could you sort it out?
We will take no further action providing...
I'll assume everything is OK unless...
I look forward to receiving your payment.

PRESENTATIONS

A Introduction

ANSWERS

2 (possible answers)
a I'm writing (in order) to update you on the current state of play.
(Why are you writing?)
b I'm calling (in order) to confirm my reservation.
(Why are you calling?)
c We should meet (in order) to discuss these figures in more detail.
(Why should we meet?)
d They reduced their prices (in order) to boost sales.
(Why did they reduce their prices?)

4 (possible answers)
We subcontrct most of our maintenance work...
a ...because we find this most cost-effective in the long term.

b ...and lease equipment rather than buy it whenever we can.
c ...although we are planning to review this shortly.
d ...but we aren't very happy with the way this is working out.

5 a to phone
b giving
c to introduce
d closing
e to hate

6 being, developing, dying, hoping, installing, paying, planning, referring, stopping, trying, using, visiting

B Preparation

KEY PHRASES

I'm (I am) calling to check what equipment you need.
Are you planning to use the video?
Do you mind using an ordinary whiteboard?

Do you have a slide projector?
I'll (I will) need a flip chart.
I'm used to working in all kinds of situations.

Is there anything else you need?
If I think of anything, I'll give you a ring.
I look forward to meeting you next week.

How does the OHP work?
How do you adjust it?
Could you get hold of an extension lead?
The OHP bulb needs changing.

How are you feeling?
Would you like a glass of water?

I'm not very keen on speaking in public.
She's (She is) very good at handling difficult questions.
He can't (cannot) stand using a microphone.
I'm not used to speaking without an OHP.
I can't get used to speaking in public.
I suppose I'll have to get used to it.

We'll (We will) begin in five minutes' time, if you're (you are) ready.
Shall I introduce you?
Good luck. I hope it goes well.

LANGUAGE NOTES

Be used to and *get used to*

Affirmative:
We are used to working late.
You will soon get used to the travelling.

Negative:
I'm not used to using an OHP.
I'll never get used to these machines.

Interrogative:
Are you used to speaking in public?
Will they get used to the new system?

Short answers:
Yes, I am.   No, I'm not.
Yes, they will.   No, they won't.

Examples:
How quickly did you get used to not having a secretary?
I can't get used to working nights.
We're not used to such a long lunch break.
She's used to handling complaints from customers!

INFORMATION

3 READING

> #### Siemens: a company statement
>
> **Orders**
>
> Siemens booked new orders worth DM63.1 billion in the period under review. This was 3% higher than the DM61.3 billion recorded a year earlier. While international orders declined 4% to DM32.8 billion (against DM34.1 billion), German orders rose 11% to DM30.3 billion (27.2 billion). This was primarily due to the high level of new orders for major systems. The largest growth was contributed by the Transportation Systems and Public Communication Networks Groups that are working on numerous projects to modernize rail and telecommunication in East Germany and other regions throughout the world. Automotive Systems grew strongly and benefited from the increasing use of electronics in automobiles.
>
> **Sales**
>
> Worldwide sales rose 8% to DM55.0 billion in the period under review (DM51.1 billion). As with orders, sales were stronger in Germany, rising 14% to DM25.9 billion (DM22.8 billion), although international sales also advanced, by 3% to DM29.1 billion (DM28.2 billion). Exports benefited from the high volume of orders received last year.
>
> **Employees**
>
> The number of employees on 30 June was about 415,000. Owing to the initial consolidation of new companies, the workforce has increased by 13,000 since the end of the fiscal year (30 September). In some areas, the workforce is being reduced to compensate for insufficient orders and changes in the company's infrastructure. The underlying figure, adjusted for the effects of initial consolidation, shows that employee numbers fell by nearly 7,000 since the start of the fiscal year. Personnel costs rose 9% to DM24.9 billion (DM22.9 billion).

Source: *The Times*, 28/7/92

ANSWERS

1 LISTENING

a flip chart	[✓]
an extension lead	[ ]
an overhead projector (OHP)	[ ]
a slide projector	[✓]
a screen	[✓]
a whiteboard	[✓]
a video recorder (VCR)	[ ]
a video camera	[ ]
a whiteboard copier	[ ]

2 LANGUAGE POINTS

1   a to   e at
    b for   f in
    c for   g in
    d of   h against

2 (possible answers)
a I don't mind answering a few questions.
b I don't enjoy giving formal presentations.
c I'm fed up with living so far from where I work.
d I can't stand listening to people's complaints.
e I'm very fond of playing squash.
f I absolutely hate having nowhere to park.
g I love working in a team.
h I sometimes don't feel like writing letters.

C Facts and figures

KEY PHRASES

These figures are based on a survey of around 19,000 people.

The graph shows the total number of unemployed workers between 1975 and 1991.
The vertical axis shows the rate of unemployment.
The year is shown on the horizontal axis.

The overall rate in 1991 was just under 9%.
At this point on the curve, there is a sharp fall.

The level of unemployment among skilled workers falls sharply here.
    skilled   unskilled   semi-skilled

That figure has gone down dramatically.
It has risen slightly.
The sales figure hasn't (has not) changed at all.
The figure for customers per day is about the same.

The figures in the left-hand column represent average sales per branch.

in the top right-hand corner
at the bottom of the page
in the final sentence
in the third bullet point

Sales average £517 per square foot.
On average, we make a sale every 3.5 seconds.
We sell twice as much as we did in 1992.
We employ half the number of staff.
Only one is three likes doing overtime.

I didn't (did not) remember to say that.
I don't (do not) remember saying that.

INFORMATION

4 READING

Partner B: Your information is more up-to-date than the information **Partner A** has. When **Partner A** calls, help him/her to update his/her records.

Marks and Spencer

- There are 283 M&S stores in the UK and Republic of Ireland.
- St Michael's is the best-selling own label brand in Britain.
- Sales average £487 per square foot.
- The flagship branch at Marble Arch hands back more money in refunds than the average M&S branch takes.
- It is visited every day by 123,000 people - more

than the capacity of a major stadium.
- Three quarters of a million garments are delivered to it every week. A delivery van of food or textiles arrives every 4.25 minutes.
- A sale is made every 3.7 seconds.
- It sells 6,500 sandwiches a day.
- It sells a ton of fresh and smoked salmon a week.

(Source: Marks and Spencer Corporate Publicity, 1993)

LANGUAGE NOTES

Verbs followed by -ing or the infinitive

Some verbs are followed by the infinitive with *to* (e.g. *expect, hope*).

e.g. I want to see the figures first.

Some verbs are followed by the infinitive without *to* (e.g. *let, make*).

e.g. Do they make you work on Saturdays?

Some verbs are followed by -ing (e.g. *enjoy, dislike, practise*).

e.g. Do you enjoy travelling on business?

Some verbs can be followed by either the infinitive with *to* or -ing; the meaning does not change significantly. Note, for instance, *hate, like, love, prefer, begin, start, continue, intend*.

e.g. She likes working.
      She likes to work.

Some verbs can be followed by either the infinitive without *to* or -ing; the meaning does not change significantly. Note, for instance, *hear, notice, see, listen, watch, feel*.

e.g. We heard him come in.
      We heard him coming in.

Some verbs can be followed by either the infinitive or -ing, and the meaning changes. Note, for instance, *stop, remember, try*.

e.g. I tried to use more visual aids.
      I tried using more visual aids.

Updating information

Note the following phrases.

e.g. That (figure) has risen/fallen a lot/little/bit.
      It has gone up/down a lot/little/bit.
      The number of deliveries is about the same as last year.
      The sales figure hasn't changed at all.
      Income hasn't changed much.

Average

As an adjective:
The average hotel stay is 1.8 nights.
The figures in the left-hand column are average sales per branch.

As a noun:
It's a table of averages for economic sectors.
On average, we make a sale every 3.5 seconds.

As a verb:
The first five months averaged an increase of 8% per month.
We average 6,000 units per month.

ANSWERS

1 LISTENING

1 a Unskilled manual
   b Junior non-manual
   c Employers and managers

2 a about nine per cent
   b 1989
   c nearly four per cent
   d skilled manual and self-employed workers

3 LANGUAGE POINTS

2 **a** There is no change of meaning.
  b Every 20 seconds, someone stops to have a cigarette.
  Every 20 seconds, someone gives up smoking.

c There is no change of meaning.
d There is no change of meaning.
e There is no change of meaning.
f I don't recall saying that.
  I forgot to say that.

D Some company presentations

KEY PHRASES

First of all, I'll (I will) give you a brief overview.
Then I'll say a few words about the takeover.

The company's main activity is selling articles produced by Mastex.
Its main purpose is to sell Mastex products.

This table shows projected sales for the coming year.
As you can see from these figures, the projected sales budget is £2 million.
Can everyone see that OK?

With regard to staffing levels, we have 20 full-time staff.
That brings me to my next point.

In 1981, Sir John King became head of the company.
In 1993, Lord King was appointed President.

Any questions so far?
Are you familiar with this terminology?

As we're (we are) running late, there's (there is) no time for more questions.
I'll hand over to Sam now because he would like to say something about our product range.
It's time for coffee, so we will have to stop there.

How did it go?
Not very well, in spite of the fact that we prepared carefully.
People couldn't hear at the back, even though I had a microphone.

LANGUAGE NOTES

Because, as and *since*

Note the following examples.

e.g. Since we're now all here, I'll begin.
  As we're running late, there's no time for more questions.
  I missed the presentation because I couldn't find a parking space.

So and *therefore*

Note the following examples.

e.g. It's time for coffee, so we will have to stop.

Our fax isn't working, so could you post it instead?
It's their responsibility. Therefore, they should pay.

(Al)though, even though, in spite of and *despite*

Note the following examples.

e.g. Although my English isn't very good, I'll try.
  Even though I had a microphone, people couldn't hear at the back.
  She is very unpopular, though I can't understand why.
  It didn't go well, in spite of the fact that we prepared carefully.
  In spite of being French, he prefers to work in the London office.
  Despite the poor results, we are optimistic for next year.

ANSWERS

1 LISTENING

1 **a** 2   **b** 1   **c** 2   **d** 1

2 The following phrases from the list on page 137 are used in the dialogues:

First presentation
First, I'll give you a brief overview of…
Then I'll say a few words about…
Any questions so far?

Second presentation
With regard to…
I'll say more about _____ in a moment.
As you can see from this table…
Can everyone see that OK?
That brings me to my next point…

2 LANGUAGE POINTS

1 **a** There is no time for more questions because we are running late.
  b Since there is no employment in this area, many people are moving abroad.
  There is no employment in this area.
  Therefore, many people are moving abroad.

135

c There was a plane strike, so we had to come by train.
   As there was a plane strike, we had to come by train.
d Since he doesn't understand English, we need an interpreter.
   He doesn't understand English, so we need an interpreter.
e Because the conference room is occupied at that time, the talk will take place in the boardroom.
   The conference room is occupied at that time. Therefore, the talk will take place in the boardroom.

2 (possible answers)
a In spite of the fact that it was brand new, the OHP didn't work.
b We were on time, even though the traffic was terrible.
c He had excellent qualifications, but he didn't get the job.

d Although I work for the company, I don't buy their products.
e Nobody placed an order, in spite of the fact that the presentation was excellent.
f Even though he is nearly 70, he works seven hours a day.
g In spite of the fact that he isn't very good at giving demonstrations, he gets excellent sales.
h Even though they have a limited product range, their turnover is huge.

3 READING

1 The notes come from a newspaper article.

2 a step down as
   b buy into or buy a stake in
   c launch
   d damages
   e anti-trust suit
   f record

FURTHER INFORMATION

SOME PHRASES USED IN MEETINGS

Getting started
Let's start.
Shall we begin?
I think we should begin.
We only have one hour.

The agenda
Can I take the minutes as read?
Has everyone got an agenda?
These are the four main topics on the agenda.
Let's start with item one.

Objectives
The main purpose of this meeting is to...
Our aim today is to...
Our main objective is to...

Introducing a topic
As you know...
I think everyone knows that...
The current situation is...
You may not know that...

Bringing people in
Mark, what's your opinion...?
Would you like to begin, Lisa, with...?
I believe you wanted to say something about...
I'd like you, John, to outline...

Points of view
I have to say that I'm opposed to...
Are you in favour of...?
I agree with that.

Moving on
Can we move on to the next item?
Let's go on to...
Can we deal with _____ next?

Digressions
Can we deal with that point later?
Can we get back to the main point?
I think we are getting away from the subject.

Concluding
Let's recap.
Is there anything anyone wants to add?
So, we have decided to...

Voting
Shall we vote on the proposal then?
Those in favour?   Those against?
Are you abstaining?

Ending the meeting
I suggest we leave it there.
Let's finish there.
I think we can call it a day.
Thank you all for coming.

SOME PHRASES USED IN PRESENTATIONS

Introducing the subject
I'm going to talk about...
The title of today's presentation is...
This talk is...

Dividing up your talk
I've divided my talk/presentation into three parts.
First (of all), I'll tell you a bit about...
First, I'll give you a brief overview of...
Then I'll say a few words about...
And finally...

Referring to a point
Regarding...   With regard to...
Concerning...   With reference to...

Referring forward
I'll say (a bit) more about that in a moment.
I'll come back to that later on.

Referring back
As I said/mentioned earlier/before...
Going back to what I said earlier...

Moving on
That brings me (on) to my next point.
Let's move on to the question of...

Referring to visuals
As you can see from this diagram/graph/table...
These figures show...
If we look at this chart...
It gives a breakdown of...

Giving examples
For instance...   For example...
Let me give you an example...

Inviting questions
Any questions so far?
Does everyone follow that?
Is that clear?
Does anyone/everyone know what _____ is?
Are you familiar with...?

Finishing off
I'd like to hand over to [Duncan Soras] now.
He is going to say a few words about...
Well, that was a brief overview of the subject.
Well, I hope that's given you some idea of...
Has anyone got any questions?
Well, if there are no more questions...
Thank you very much for your attention.

Asking for clarification
Can I ask a question?
Could you just say a bit more about...?
What exactly do/did you mean by...?
Could you explain what _____ is once again?
I didn't understand what you said about...

Problems
Can everyone see that [transparency] OK?
It's not in focus.   It's out of focus.
Can you hear me at the back?
I've forgotten what I was going to say.
It's completely gone out of my head.

FURTHER INFORMATION FOR UNIT 1B

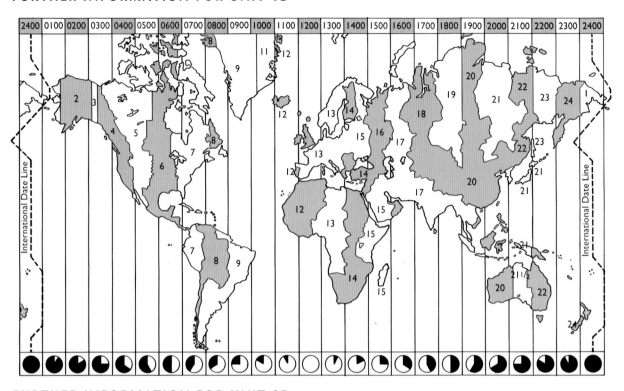

FURTHER INFORMATION FOR UNIT 2B

Complete and return to:
The Manager, Commercial Banking Services, National Westminster Bank, FREEPOST Hounslow TW4 5BR.

This information is requested to ensure that future **PHAROS** developments accurately reflect the needs of those using the system. It will not be used for any unrelated mailing activity and will remain absolutely confidential.

For internal use only

1 Name
Title   First Name   Surname

Position
Business Name
Business Address

Postcode
Telephone Number

2 Type of Business
Sole Proprietor ☐   PLC ☐
Partnership ☐   Subsidiary ☐
Private Limited Company ☐   Other ☐

3 Turnover
Up to £250,000 ☐   £1m-£5m ☐
£250,000-£1m ☐   £5m+ ☐

4 Currently involved in import/export
Export only ☐   Import and export ☐
Import only ☐   None ☐

5 Number of companies/divisions
1-2 ☐   3-6 ☐   6+ ☐

6 Number of employees
1-9 ☐   31-100 ☐
10-30 ☐   100+ ☐

7 Is your company
NatWest Customer ☐   Member of CBI ☐
Emst & Young Client ☐   Other ☐

8 Please indicate your company's main business activities
Agriculture, forestry and fishing ☐
Energy and water supply ☐
Mining, chemicals ☐
Metal goods, engineering, vehicles ☐
Electronics ☐
Other manufacturing industries ☐
Construction ☐
Retail, distribution, hotels, catering, repairs ☐
Transport, communications ☐
Banking, financial, business services ☐
Education, health, government and local authorities ☐
Other ☐

9 Bankers
NatWest ☐   Barclays ☐   Midland ☐
Lloyds ☐   RBS ☐   Other ☐

10 Disk size required
3½" ☐   5¼" ☐

Copyright in PHAROS is the joint property of National Westminster Bank PLC and Emst and Young.
You will be licensed to use PHAROS on a single computer only for your internal business purposes, but not for the provision of information or advice to third parties. PHAROS may not be copied, save for any transient copies necessarily created by using PHAROS. You may not modify, de-compile or disassemble PHAROS.
PHAROS is supplied "as is" without warranties of any kind. PHAROS is intended as general guidance only. On any specific matter reference should be made to an appropriate professional adviser.

Signature _____
Date _____

LIST OF IRREGULAR VERBS

Infinitive	Past Tense	Past Participle
be	was/were	been
bear	bore	born
become	became	become
begin	began	begun
break	broke	broken
bring	brought	brought
build	built	built
burn	burnt/burned	burnt/burned
buy	bought	bought
catch	caught	caught
choose	chose	chosen
come	came	come
cost	cost	cost
cut	cut	cut
deal	dealt	dealt
do	did	done
drink	drank	drunk
drive	drove	driven
eat	ate	eaten
fall	fell	fallen
feed	fed	fed
feel	felt	felt
find	found	found
fly	flew	flown
forget	forgot	forgotten
get	got	got (US gotten)
give	gave	given
go	went	gone
grow	grew	grown
have	had	had
hear	heard	heard
hold	held	held
hurt	hurt	hurt
keep	kept	kept
know	knew	known
lead	led	led

Infinitive	Past Tense	Past Participle
learn	learnt	learnt
leave	left	left
lend	lent	lent
let	let	let
lose	lost	lost
make	made	made
mean	meant	meant
meet	met	met
pay	paid	paid
put	put	put
read	read	read
ring	rang	rung
rise	rose	risen
run	ran	run
say	said	said
see	saw	seen
sell	sold	sold
send	sent	sent
set	set	set
show	showed	shown
shut	shut	shut
sit	sat	sat
sleep	slept	slept
speak	spoke	spoken
spell	spelt	spelt
spend	spent	spent
stand	stood	stood
swim	swam	swum
take	took	taken
teach	taught	taught
tell	told	told
think	thought	thought
understand	understood	understood
wear	wore	worn
win	won	won
write	wrote	written

WORD LIST

A

abroad (1)
abstain (7)
abstention (7)
a/c = account (9)
account (5)
accountancy (9)
accountant (1)
account for (2) *Sales accounted for 97% of national consumption.*
account number (9)
accounts (9)
accreditation (7)
acquisition (2)
action (7) *action point, action step*
action (9) *to take no further action*
activity (2)
actuary (3)
adjust (10)
admin = administration (2)
administrator (1)
advance (6) *to advance an idea*
advance (7) *to circulate the agenda in advance*
advanced (2) *technologically very advanced*
advertisement (4)
advertising (3)
afford (6)
after-sales service (4)
against (1) *Time is against us.*
against (7) *I'm against the proposal.*
agenda (1)
agent (1)
AGM = annual general meeting (9)
agree to (6)
agricultural (8) *agricultural region*
ahead (1) *three hours ahead of us*
aim (7)
aluminium (4)
Amex = American Express (8)
amount (9)
analyst (5) *business analyst, systems analyst*
annually (5)
answer machine (1)
anti-trust suit (10)
AOB = any other business (7)
apologies (7)
applicants (5)
appointments (3)
approved by (7)
APR = annual percentage rate (9)
arrangements (1)
arrival (8)

assets (9)
assistant (1)
article (7) *newspaper article*
article (10) *We sell articles produced by Mastex.*
attn. = attention (8) *for the attention of*
audit (9)
authorised (9)
authorities (5)
automation (1)
available (7)
average (10)
axis (10)

B

back (7) *on our backs*
bad debts (9)
bal. = balance (9)
ban (7) *a ban on smoking, to ban smoking*
bank (1)
based (2) *Where are you based?*
based on (10) *These figures are based on a survey of 15,000 people.*
batch (5)
barrister (5)
bear (4) *We will bear the cost.*
behalf (8) *on behalf of*
behind (1) *three hours behind*
b/f = brought forward / bring forward (9)
benefit (10) *Exports benefited from a high volume of orders overseas.*
bid (10) *Their bid to buy into the company failed.*
bill (8) *Please send the bill to Rembola Ltd.*
biotechnology (8)
block (2) *the admin block*
board (8) *to board an aircraft*
board meeting (10)
boardroom (7)
bonus scheme (3)
bonnet (4) *car bonnet*
book (6) *She is booking hospitality at a golf tournament.*
book (9) *book value*
book (10) *They booked new orders worth DM63.1 billion.*
book into (5) *Why did you book me into that hotel?*
bookkeeper (10)
boom (10) *the eighties boom*
boost (10) *We want to boost sales.*
boss (1)

bought ledger (9)
brand (10) *brand name, own brand*
brand (10) *brand new*
branch (1) *She liaises with all the company branches.*
break down (4) *It has broken down twice already.*
break into (9) *Our home was broken into.*
bring forward (9)
brochure (1)
broker (5) *stock broker, insurance broker*
budget (7)
bulk (5) *bulk plastic packaging*
bumper (4) *The bumper is loose.*
business (1) *the construction business*
business analyst (5)
business card (6)
buy in (2) *EDF buys in some of its production.*
buy into (10) *They wanted to buy into United Airways.*
buyout (2) *management buyout*

C

calculate (9)
call back (1)
call off (7)
call-out (5) *emergency call-outs*
cancel (7)
canteen (7)
capital goods (8)
car hire (1)
caretaking staff (5)
carousel type projector (10)
carry forward (9) *balance carried forward*
cash (9) *cash a cheque, pay in cash*
cash dispenser (9)
casing (4) *The casing is made of plastic.*
casual (6)
catalogue number (4)
catering (5)
chair (7) *Owen should chair the meeting.*
chairman (2) *the Chairman of the Board of Directors*
charge (4) *The prices they charge are very reasonable.*
charge (5) *free of charge*
charge (7) *in charge*
chart (10)
chartered accountant (3)
check (8) *Can I check my bags through to Dublin?*

check-in (8)
cheers (6)
chemicals (8)
cheque (9) *by cheque*
chief (2) *chief accountant, chief executive*
circulate (7)
claim (5) *make a claim under the terms of your guarantee, insurance claim*
claims manager (5)
clear (9) *clear an overdraft/debt*
clerical (3)
clerk (3)
clients (1)
close down (3)
co. = company (9)
collaboration (2)
colleagues (1)
column (10)
come into effect (7) *At midnight, a new law will come into effect.*
come off it (7)
come over (7) *Some people are coming over from Mexico.*
come up (3) *Something has come up.*
commercial (1) *commercial loans*
commission (5)
committee (7)
company car (2)
company secretary (5)
company tie (5)
compensation (7)
compete with (1)
competitor (1)
complaint (1)
component (4)
computer (1)
concrete (8) *reinforced concrete*
conference (3)
confirm (1)
conglomerate (2)
connection (9) *in connection with*
consignment (5)
consolidation (10)
construct (4)
construction business (1)
consult (4)
consultancy (5)
consumable (5)
consumption (2)
contact (1) *business contact, make contact with someone*
contact (1) *Ask him to contact me.*
contract (1)
contract out (5)
controller (1)
convenient (7)
conveyancing (2)

co-operation (7)
co-ordinating (1)
co-ordinator (10)
copier (10)
copy (7) *a copy of the agenda*
corporate (3)
cost (9)
cost-effective (5)
course (5) *training course*
course (6) *first course, main course*
cover (1) *to cover the points, to cover ground*
cover for (9) *Are you covered for theft?*
crate (4)
creche (5)
credit card (8)
credit control (4)
credit limit (7)
creditor (9)
currency (2)
current (9) *current account*
curve (10) *At this point on the curve...*
customer (1) *customer base*
customise (4)
cut (5) *to cut costs*

D

daily (5)
data processing systems (1)
damages (10) *to pay £3.5m in damages*
day-to-day (3)
deadline (1)
deal (1) *to get a cheap deal*
deal in (1)
deal with (4) *They deal with catering.*
dealings (1)
debtor (9)
decline (10) *The number of orders declined.*
defer (9) *deferred taxation*
delay (7) *The meeting has been delayed till 3.15.*
delivery (3)
delivery charges (4)
demand (4)
demanding (1) *demanding customers*
demonstration (10)
dept. = department (1)
departure (8)
deposit (5) *to pay a deposit*
depot (5)
depreciation (9)
design (4) *a popular design, design department*
despatch (5) *It was despatched today.*

details (1)
Deutsch Mark (2)
dictate (5) *I was dictating a memo.*
dinner dance (3)
direct (7) *direct from Brussels, direct export operation*
direct debit (9)
direct number (1)
director (2)
disk (2)
discontinue (4) *That line is discontinued.*
discount (5)
dispenser (8)
distribution (2)
diversification (10)
diversified (2) *a diversified company*
divide into (10) *I've divided the talk into three parts.*
dividend (9)
division (2) *The company has four divisions.*
do (6) *an evening do*
dollar (2)
domestic (9)
down (3) *A machine is down.*
down (9) *Our personal expenditure is down.*
downside (5)
draw up (7) *to draw up a plan*
drink to (6)
due (9)
durable (4)
duty (9) *to pay duty*

E

earn (9)
economic (8) *economic area, economic climate*
ECU = European Currency Unit (9)
efficiently (6)
electronic (2)
emergency (5)
employee (1)
encl. = enclosed (7)
end (7) *at my end*
engaged (1) *The line is engaged.*
engineering (1)
enquiry (4)
enrol (5)
entertaining (6)
entry (9) *an entry on a bank statement*
environment (1) *business environment*
equal (7) *senior, junior or equal in position*
equipment (1)

establish (1) *to establish good relationships, to establish something as a rule*
estimate (1)
ETA = estimated time of arrival (8)
ex-boss (3)
exchange rate (9)
executive (1)
exhibition (1)
expand (3)
expansion (9)
expect (8) *I expect I'll still be here.*
expenditure (5)
expense (6) *a business expense*
expenses (5) *My fee is £3000, plus expenses.*
exploit (2)
export (2)
ext. = extension (number) (1)
extension lead (10)
extra charge (5)

F

fabric (4)
facilities (1)
facsimile machine (5)
factor (9)
factory (1)
faithfully (8) *Yours faithfully*
fall apart (4) *equipment that falls apart staightaway*
far off (3) *I'm not far off retirement age.*
favour (7) *in favour of*
fax (1)
fee (5)
figure (5)
filing (2) *to do the filing*
finalise (8)
finance (1)
financial (2)
fire (3) *to fire someone*
firm (2)
fiscal (10) *fiscal year*
fixed assets (9)
fixed price (5)
flagship (10)
flight (8)
flip chart (10)
floppy drive (5)
fold (4) *The panel edge is folded.*
force (1) *a large sales force*
foreign (6)
formula (9)
forward (4) *Please forward details of your range of products.*
found (2) *The company was founded in 1967.*
founder member (8)
frame (4) *The frame is connected by wires.*

free (6)
free of charge (5)
French franc (2)
fringe benefit (3)
full-time (3)
fully (6) *fully booked*
funds (9) *Have you transferred the funds?*

G

gas station (2)
gauge (4) *petrol gauge*
GDP = gross domestic product (8)
gear (8) *cold-weather gear*
gearbox (4)
gearstick (4)
get hold of (1)
get in touch with (1)
get on (7) *How are you getting on with it?*
get out of (7) *a commitment that I can't get out of*
get round to (9) *They haven't got round to paying it yet.*
get something done (7)
get through (4) *I've been trying to get through for an hour.*
get together (7) *When can we get together?*
give out (1) *We don't give out private numbers.*
give up (7) *to give up smoking*
glass (4)
GNP = gross national product (9)
goods (4)
go ahead (5) *Go ahead – tell me.*
go down (10) *That figure has gone down dramatically.*
go off (3) *The alarm went off.*
go over (7) *go over some papers*
go up (5) *I'm afraid our rates have gone up.*
grade (5) *We sort and grade them.*
graph (10)
group (7)
gross (9)
growth (10)
guarantee (2) *to guarantee continued production*
guest (6)

H

hand back (10)
handle (4) *Our department doesn't handle this.*
handout (10)
hand over (5)
hard disk (5)
hardware (1)
haulage contractor (1)

head (1) *head of the legal department*
headlamp (4)
heavy-duty (4)
here's to (6)
hire (5)
hold (6) *It might be difficult to hold the booking till then.*
hold (7) *to hold a meeting*
hold on (1) *Could you hold on while I go and get her.*
horizontal (10)
hospitality (6) *business hospitality*
hotel industry (5)
hourly-paid (7)
hours (1) *office hours*
HQ = headquarters (9)
human resources (2)

I

implement (7) *to implement a change*
import (2)
income (9)
inc. = incorporated (8)
increase (7) *Our main aim is to approve the budget increases.*
increase (9) *We increased profits by 15%.*
incur (6) *to incur an expense*
industrial (4)
industry (8)
informal (6)
information (1)
information technology (5)
infrastructure (10)
in-house (5)
in-service (5)
installation (5)
insurance (5)
insurance broker (5)
insurance salesman (5)
insured (9)
interest (9) *a high interest account*
interest rate (9)
internal (1)
international (10)
interrupt (6)
investor (5)
investment (2)
invoice (5)
IOU = I owe you (9)
issue (6)
IT = information technology (5)
item (4)
itinerary (4)

J

jet lag (8)
joint venture (8)
judge (5)

junior (7)

K

keep my head above water (7)
keep someone happy (2)
keep straight (3) *to keep files straight*
key factor (9)
keyboard (3)

L

label (10)
labour (5)
laminating (2) *a laminating line*
laminator (2)
lap-top (2)
launch (10) *to launch a survival plan*
law (5)
lawyer (1)
lead (10) *extension lead*
leadership (5)
leaflet (1)
lease (5)
ledger (9)
legal department (1)
letter of introduction (1)
level (10) *staffing levels*
liabilities (9)
liaise (3)
liaison (3)
lift (7) *to give someone a lift*
line (1) *on another line*
line (4) *We have discontinued that line.*
load (4) *The loads are suspended below.*
loan (7)
locally (4) *It's manufactured locally.*
locate (9) *I'll try and locate the invoice.*
locate (9) *Where are they going to locate the new plant?*
located (6) *conveniently located*
location (2)
long-haul (8) *long-haul flight*
look forward to (1) *I look forward to meeting you.*
look into (9) *I'll look into it for you.*
lot (5) *the lot*
lunchbreak (10)

M

machine (8)
machinery (2)
make (1) *Well done – you made it.*
made to order (4)
mailing (2)

mail order (2)
main (8) *main office*
maintenance (1)
make a claim (9)
make clear (5)
make the meeting (7)
make a toast (6)
make up your mind (4)
management (9)
manager (1)
managing director (2)
manual (3) *manual worker*
manual (9) *training manual*
manufacturer (2)
manufacturing (8) *manufacturing industry*
marked (8) *marked for the attention of*
marker pen (10)
marketing (4)
market (2)
market position (2)
market researcher (1)
market value (10)
margin (4) *narrow margin*
Mastercard (8)
material (5)
matter (1) *This is a matter of urgency.*
measure (9) *to measure performance*
MD = managing director (7)
media (9)
medical instrument (1)
meet (9) *to meet a challenge, to meet a need*
meeting (1)
meet up (7)
memo (3)
message (1)
mess someone around (7)
metallurgy (8)
micro-electronics (8)
middle (1) *I'm in the middle of something.*
middle manager (3)
mining (2)
minutes (7)
mobile number (1)
model number (4)
modernise (10)
monopoly (2)
monthly (5)
motivation (5)
move (3) *to move house*

N

nationalise (2) *nationalised industry*
net (5) *net total*

network (2)
NIC = national insurance contributions (9)
non-manual (10)

O

off the shelf (4)
office (1)
offshore (8) *offshore oil and gas*
OHP = overhead projector (10)
oil (8)
one-off (5) *on a one-off basis*
operate (1)
operating profit (9)
operative craftsman (3)
opposed (7) *I'm opposed to spending more money on this.*
order (7)
order number (1)
organise (6) *She organised it brilliantly.*
organisation (8)
o/s = outstanding (9)
outgoings (9)
outlet (2)
outline (7)
out of date (10)
output (2)
outright purchase (5)
outside (1) *outside office hours*
outside contractor (5)
outstanding (9)
over (1) *Let's discuss it over a drink.*
over (6) *When foreign clients are over in London...*
overall (3) *Why don't you wear an overall?*
overall (9) *overall revenue*
overcharge (5)
overdraft (9)
overdraw (9) *My account is overdrawn.*
overhead transparency (10)
overrun (7)
overseas (1)
overtime (1)
overview (2)
owe (8)

P

PA = personal assistant (9)
package (3) *redundancy package, hospitality package*
pallet (5)
panel (4) *The fabric is cut into panels.*
paperwork (8)
parent company (2)
partner (8)

partnership (2)
part-time (3)
pay (8) *I'd like to pay by Visa.*
PAYE = pay as you earn (9)
payment (9)
pay off (7) *to pay off a loan*
peak (10) *to reach a peak*
peak (10) *The rate of unemployment peaked in 1987.*
PC = personal computer (2)
pension contribution (3)
pension plan (9)
people (1) *maintenance people*
per (5) *per annum, per passenger*
per cent (8)
performance (9)
period (9)
perks (2)
personnel (2)
peseta (2)
petrochemicals (8)
pharmaceuticals (4)
photocopier (1)
pick up (4) *I'll send a car to pick you up.*
pick up the tab (6) *My boss will pick up the tab.*
pie chart (10)
PIN = personal identity number (9)
plant (1)
plastics (4)
PLC = public limited company (2)
plough back (9) *to plough profits back*
point (7) *I agree up to a point.*
point (7) *We didn't manage to cover all the points.*
police (5)
policy (2) *protectionist policy*
policy (5) *insurance policy*
post (9) *It was sent by post.*
postage (9)
postpone (7)
potential (7)
pound (2)
power station (2)
PR = public relations (9)
premises (6)
premium (9)
prepare (1)
present (7) *Everyone was present.*
presentation (4)
president (8)
pressure (1) *under a lot of pressure*
price (2)
price list (4)
pricing formula (9)
printer (5)
private health insurance (3)

private number (1) *We don't give out private numbers.*
privatisation (2)
procedure (7)
process (9) *to process an invoice*
processing (8) *food processing*
producer (4)
product (1)
production (1)
productivity (9)
professional (10)
profit (1)
profitably (9)
programmer (5) *computer programmer*
project (1) *a new project*
projected (7) *projected R&D spending*
projector (10) *slide projector, overhead projector*
promote (3) *He was promoted to production director.*
promotion (8)
proposal (7)
propose a toast (6)
proprietor (2) *sole proprietor*
prospective (4)
protectionist (2)
PTO = please turn over (9)
public utility (2)
publicity (5)
publicly owned (2)
purchasing (1)
purpose-built (5)
put (5) *Let me put it another way.*
put (6) *Put the drinks on my bill.*
put off (7) *The meeting has been put off till Tuesday.*
put right (4)
put someone through (3) *Why do I put myself through all this?*
put through (1) *I'll put you through.*
put to (7) *I'll put it to him.*

Q

qualified (3) *a qualified accountant*
quality (2)
quantity (9)
quantity surveyor (3)
quarter (3) *Profit fell in the last quarter.*
quarterly (5)
quarters (7) *from some quarters*
query (9)
quote (5)

R

R&D = research and development (2)
raise the matter (7)
rank (2)
range (1) *a range of products*
rate (9) *to agree a rate*
rates (5) *Their rates have gone up.*
re. = referring to (6)
reach (1) *I don't know how to reach you.*
real estate (9)
recall (4)
recap (7)
receipt (9)
receive (9)
reception (1) *There's a visitor in reception for you.*
reception (6) *The reception went well.*
receptionist (6)
recession (2)
recipient (9)
record (10) *record profits*
recorded (10)
records (9) *You'll find it in your records.*
reduction (7)
redundant (3)
reference number (4)
refining (1) *refining facilities*
refund (5)
regards (8) *Send her my regards.*
region (10)
registration (9)
regulation (5) *safety regulations*
reinforce (4) *The joins are reinforced by tapes.*
relationship (8)
relocate (2)
remuneration (9)
rental (5)
reorder (5)
rep = representative (3)
repair (5)
repay (9)
replace (5)
reply (6)
report (7) *a report on the new computer system*
report to (1) *staff who report to you*
represent (10)
representative (2)
reservation (6) *I want to confirm my reservation.*
resign (3)
responsible for (1)
results (9)
retailing (9) *retailing revenue per passenger*

retail price index (9)
retire (3)
revaluation reserve (9)
revenue (9)
review (7) *a review of the budget*
rip off (5) *We don't rip people off.*
rise (6) *Sales rose slowly.*
risk (5) *an insurance policy to cover all risks*
room (1) *room for improvement*
room (6) *That would leave us room for afternoon tea.*
round (6) *round of drinks*
routine (5)
RPI = retail price index (9)
run (9) *computer run*
run (1) *run a company, run a car*
run (6) *run smoothly*
run (5) *run low, run late*
run out of (10)
run through (8)

S

salaried (2)
sales (1)
salesman (4)
salesperson (6)
sample (1)
savings (9)
scheduled (6)
screen (3)
secretary (3)
sector (10)
security (5)
security guard (5)
see someone off (7)
self-employed (3)
sell (1)
semi-skilled (10)
senior (7)
sensor (2)
service (1) *provide a service*
service (4) *This machine ought to be serviced.*
service (6) *Service is included.*
service charge (5)
service contract (5)
service industries (5)
set aside (7)
set a target (9)
set up (7) *to set up a meeting*
settle (9) *to settle a payment*
settlement (9)
sew (4) *The fabric is sewn together.*
sewage plant (2)
shake hands (6)
share certificate (5)
shareholder (9)
share (2) *stocks and shares*
sharp (1) *four o'clock sharp*
sheet of paper (1)

shipbuilding (8)
shop floor (3)
show up (6) *Don't show up late.*
show round (7) *I have to show them round.*
shuttle (3)
sick leave (1)
sign (8)
signature (5)
sincerely (8) *Yours sincerely*
single market (2)
site (2)
sit through (3) *Have you ever had to sit through a sales conference?*
skilled (3) *skilled worker*
slide projector (10)
slow down (3) *Her bad back slows her down a bit.*
software (1)
sole proprietor (2)
solicitor (2)
solution (1) *a solution to a problem*
sort out (1)
sound (7) *How does that sound?*
spare part (5)
spare time (1)
specialise in (2)
spending (7)
spend on (9) *We spend very little on holidays.*
split (6) *to split the bill*
staff (1)
staffing (10)
stake (10) *to buy a stake in*
stand (1) *exhibition stand*
stand (4) *to stand the usage it gets*
stand for (8) *What does LAFTA stand for?*
standard (1)
staple (4) *They are stapled together.*
star (8) *two-star hotel*
statement (9)
state of play (10)
state-owned (2)
stationery (1)
stay on the fence (7)
stay over (6) *Does he plan to stay over the weekend?*
steel (8) *stainless steel*
step down (10) *He stepped down as chairman to become president.*
stock (9) *current stock*
stock (4) *in stock, out of stock*
stock (4) *Do you still stock that model?*
stock (9) *stocks and shares*
stock broker (5)
stock dealer (5)
Stock Exchange (9)
stock market (5)
stockist (4)

store (10) *a high street store*
storeroom (2)
strategy (9)
street corner supplier (5)
strike (7) *to go on strike*
stuck (3)
stuff (5)
subcontract (5)
subcontractor (5)
subscription (9)
subsidiary (2)
subsidise (5)
subsidy (2)
sundry (9) *sundry expenses, sundry items*
superiors (1)
supplier (1)
surplus (9)
survey (9)
switchboard (1)
switch off (5)
systems analyst (5)

T

tab (6) *to pick up the tab*
table (10)
take apart (4) *to take a machine apart*
take care of (7)
take delivery (5)
take someone for a ride (7)
take time off (6)
take up time (3)
takeover (10)
talk through (7)
target (9)
tax advisor (1)
taxation (9)
team (6)
terms of trading (9)
technical (1)
technology (8)
technologically (2)
telephone system (5)
tenant (9)
terms (4) *delivery terms*
textile (8) *textile industry*
tie up with (9)
tied up (1) *I'm a bit tied up right now.*
tight (1) *Money is tight.*
time (1) *2 pm your time*
tip (6)
token (7) *to pay a token amount*
total (9) *total price, total revenue*
touch (7) *in touch*
tour (9) *away on tour*
tourism (1)
trade (3)
trading (9) *in accordance with our terms of trading*

trainee (9)
training (2)
transfer (8) *transfer by car to Ipoh, transfer desk*
transfer (8) *technology transfer*
transfer (9) *to transfer funds*
transit (8) *in transit*
transmission (2)
transmit (8) *Our fax machine isn't transmitting properly.*
transparency (10)
traveller's cheque (9)
trend (10)
turnover (2)
turnpike (8)
typing (2) *do the typing*

U

underlying (10) *the underlying figure adjusted for the effects of restructuring*
unemployed (3)
unemployment (10)
union rep (7)

unskilled (10) *unskilled worker*
update (5)
up (9) *Expenditure is up.*
up to (3) *What are you up to these days?*
up-to-date (10)
user (5)

V

vacancy (6) *Do you have any vacancies next week?*
value (8)
VAT = value added tax (5)
VCR = video recorder (10)
video (10)
VIP = very important person (6)
Visa (8)
visitor (1)
volume (10)
vote (7)

W

waiver (8)

warehouse (2)
water works (2)
weekly (5)
wire (4) *stainless steel wires*
whiteboard (10)
workforce (2)
worker (7)
work for (3) *Who were you working for?*
work on (3) *What were you working on?*
work out (6) *The plan didn't work out.*
working parts (4)
work-related (6)
works manager (3)
workshop (5)
worldwide (10)
worth (5)

Y

yen (2)

GRAMMAR INDEX